Stirring Slur. ɡ

250 Eucharistic Reflections

Compiled and Edited

by

Mr. Michael Seagriff, O.P.

Stirring Slumbering Souls

250 Eucharistic Reflections

Copyright © 2017 by Michael Seagriff

ISBN-13: -978-0578198569
ISBN-10: 0578198568

Disclaimer: The ideas expressed in this book are those of the author alone and do not represent the endorsement or position of the Lay Fraternities of St. Dominic or the Order of Preachers as a whole.

Photography: Front cover image and all interior photographs by Mr. Michael Seagriff, O.P.

Printed in the United States of America

Michael Seagriff
Canastota, New York

Dedication

In reparation to our loving and merciful Lord imprisoned in the tabernacles of His churches where He is far too often abandoned, disrespected, forgotten and ignored.

Mary, our Mother, lead us into the Eucharistic embrace of Your Son, Our Lord Jesus Christ.

Table of Contents

...to the Real Presence of Jesus, we often respond
with our real absence!

Father Florian Racine

Introduction

Are your hearts hardened? Do you have eyes, but fail to see? Do you have ears, but fail to hear?

(Matthew 16:17-18)

Have you ever loved someone so much that you could hardly wait to hear from them, speak with them and see them? How often have you looked forward to a visit from someone you deeply love only to have that person not come? How hurt have you felt when you were ignored and your love not returned?

Imagine then how God - Who is Love - Who loves us more than words can describe - feels when we fail to demonstrate our love for Him. He waits, hour after hour in our churches, behind locked tabernacle doors, as a Prisoner of Love, just to hear our voices and see our faces.

Few of us come to be with Him. Many no longer believe He is really and substantially present in the Sacred Eucharist. For all practical purposes, He is abandoned, ignored and disrespected.

This despite the fact: that God the Father on Mount Tabor commanded Peter, James, John and all who would later hear of Jesus' Transfiguration *to listen to His Son.*; that Jesus Himself later scolded the same three apostles for their failure *to watch one hour with Him*; and that His Blessed Mother directed the servants at Cana and all who would later learn of this miracle *to do whatever Jesus tells them.*

We have not listened to God the Father. We have not obeyed His Son. We have not heeded the Blessed Mother.

We have taken God for granted. We have failed to love our Lord as we ought and as He deserves.

Despite our deafness and disobedience, Jesus never gives up on us.

From time to time, He prompts others to "shake things up." This book attempts to do just that.

As you read and ponder the content of this book, may you recognize, as Father Bruno Shah, O.P. has suggested to me, two distinct voices – "the prophet calling Israel back to fidelity" and "the sweet Mother inviting us to trust in Her Son."

****

In Matthew's Gospel (8:23-34) the evangelist tells us that when Jesus crossed over from Galilee into the mostly Gentile area of the Gadarenes. He and His disciples approached a field where a large herd of swine were feeding. There Jesus encountered two demon possessed men who made travel on this particular road impossible.

The demons within these men immediately recognized Jesus as the Son of God. It had to be excruciatingly painful for these evil spirits to remain in His Presence. They begged Jesus to send them into the nearby herd of swine.

"Out with you!" Jesus commanded. They entered the swine and the entire herd ran down the bluff and into the sea where they drowned.

At this sight, the swine's caretakers (herdsmen), not knowing who Jesus was or understanding what they had just witnessed, fled the area and informed their fellow townspeople what they had seen. Matthew tells us that everyone in the town later came back to meet Jesus.

They came. They saw Jesus. But did they actually meet Him?

The townsfolk had to have seen the formerly possessed men now normal in appearance and behavior. One would think they would be full of gratitude for their restoration, to be rid of these evil spirits and to be able to travel freely on the road without fear or impediment. Surely, if they really wanted to meet and thank this Man, they would spend time in His presence, talking with and listening to Him. They had to have a multitude of questions: Who was He? From whence came His power to cast out demons? Why did He come to their town? - and so on and on.

The Son of God was in their midst! He came there intentionally. Although they were Gentiles, He was ready to welcome them into His loving embrace. He who had cast out demons was ready to transform them. They failed to recognize Who He was and how blessed they were to be in His Presence. They showed Him no appreciation, reverence or respect. They asked no questions. They sought no relationship with Him.

Instead, they let fear take root and snuff out the offer of faith and salvation standing at their feet. Through their actions and words, they did the unthinkable – they told Him, the Second Person of the Blessed Trinity, the Savior of mankind, the Son of God, that He was not welcome in their town, their hearts or their souls. They begged God to leave!

He left. God would never interfere with anyone's free will no matter the pain their poor choices caused His Most Sacred and Merciful Heart.

How tragic! Jesus was right there, in their midst, seeking a relationship with each of them. They were not interested!

But let's not be too quick to condemn or cast stones at these blind souls.

Have not many of us treated Jesus in a similar manner as did the Gadarenes – not taking the time to meet, talk and listen to Him? Are we just as reluctant to seek a relationship with Him, as were they? How many of us act like Jesus is not really, truly and substantially present here with us in the Eucharist? Do we act irreverently toward Him? Do we ignore Him, content to abandon Him to His tabernacle-prison?

If we do go to Church are we anxious to get out as quickly as we can? Do we spend time expressing our gratitude for the Gift of His Presence? Do we prepare ourselves properly to receive His Body, Blood, Soul and Divinity and with the awe, amazement, and gratitude such a Gift deserves?

How many of us ever come back to visit and talk to Him during the week? When is the last time we spent time in His Presence, just sitting there silently, basking in the invisible but ever-present graces flowing from behind the locked tabernacle doors or from the Sacred and Most Precious monstrance in which He hides Himself humbly behind the Consecrated Host?

The truth is that we are all guilty of inattention, indifference and irreverence toward the God Who lives among us and wishes to live within us.

To have the Son of God here with us and not to spend time with Him is the same as telling Him that we are not interested in getting to know or have an intimate relationship with Him and that He is not welcome in our minds, hearts or souls. Like the Gadarenes, we are telling the Son of God we do not want Him in, or to interfere with, our lives. We are telling God we are not interested - to leave.

When we act this way, are we not just like the nine lepers who were healed but never returned to thank Jesus?

Is not our lack of belief, indifference, irreverence, ingratitude and neglect of our Lord a far more violent affront to His Most Precious, Sacred, and Mystical Heart than was the physical lance the Roman centurion Longinus thrust into His lifeless side?

****

As the undeserving beneficiaries of God's forgiveness, mercy, and love, how have we expressed our gratitude to Him? There are 168 hours in each week. Certainly, we can find some time to be in His Presence, adore Him, talk to Him, listen to Him, and make reparation to Him for the countless indignities and blasphemies He endures.

We just have to love God enough to gift our time to Him.

May our loving and waiting Lord use the 250 quotations in this book to increase belief in, reverence for, devotion to and love of His Eucharistic Presence, touch lukewarm hearts, stir slumbering souls, and re-ignite the flame of love for Him that He placed in our hearts the second He breathed life into them.

Listen to Him speak as you read and ponder these truths. Take a close look at yourself. Recognize the many ways in which you offend Him daily. Feel His pain and anguish over being abandoned and ignored and treated irreverently. Understand how thirsty He is for your love.

Then love and treat Him as He deserves.

****

"The cure for all the spiritual cancer and evils in the world is Jesus Christ and His wonderful Presence in the Blessed Sacrament...We all need Eucharistic Adoration in our lives if we ever hope to make it safely into the harbor of Heaven."

(Father Daniel Doctor)

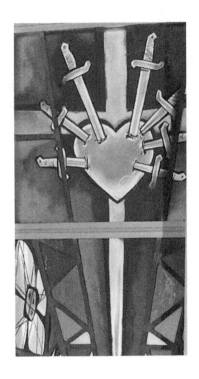

Our swords of ingratitude painfully pierce His Most Sacred Heart.

QUOTATIONS

By means of the angels, Jesus calls the poor and simple shepherds, in order to manifest Himself to them. He calls the learned men by means of their science. And all of them, moved by His inner grace, hasten to adore Him. He calls all of us by Divine inspiration, and communicates with us by means of His grace. How many times has He invited us, too? And how readily have we responded? My God, I blush and become embarrassed when I have to answer such a question.

(Saint Padre Pio)

Does not God who remains in the world under the Species of bread, Who empties Himself to such a degree, merit a limitless love in return?

(Saint Maximilian Kolbe)

Ah! if we had the eyes of angels with which to see Our Lord Jesus Christ, who is here present on this altar, and who is looking at us, how we should love Him! We should never more wish to part from Him. We should wish to remain always at His feet; it would be a foretaste of Heaven: all else would become insipid to us. But see, it is faith we want. We are poor blind people; we have a mist before our eyes. Faith alone can dispel this mist. Presently, my children, when I shall hold Our Lord in my hands, when the good God blesses you, ask Him then to open the eyes of your heart; say to Him like the blind man of Jericho, 'O Lord, make me to see!' If you say to Him sincerely, 'Make me to see!' you will certainly obtain what you desire, because He wishes nothing but your happiness. He has His hands full of graces, seeking to whom to distribute them; Alas! and no one will have them…Oh, indifference! Oh, ingratitude! My children, we are most unhappy that we do not understand these things! We shall understand them well one day; but it will then be too late!

(Saint John Vianney)

I wait for my priests. I long to see them enter my sanctuary and approach the tabernacle of My abiding presence. I wait for them in the Sacrament that I left for their sakes as the expression of my Divine friendship for my priests, as their consolation in loneliness, their strength in weakness, their sweetness in life's bitterness.

When my priests seek My company, I am moved to show them the compassionate love of my Heart. When they draw near to Me it is because I have already drawn near to them, set My gaze upon them, given them My Heart's love of predilection, and claimed them for Myself and for My Bride, the Church.

If they come in search of my Eucharistic Face, it is because the light of My Face has already illumined their darkness. Some see the light of My Face and walk in its radiance. Others see it and turn away, choosing darkness over My light. Even among my priests there are those who forsake the light of My Face for the demon-infested darkness that will lead to their destruction.

How I grieve over those of My priests who turn from me. How I grieve over those of My priests who pretend not to have seen My light nor to have recognized My Face. These, like Peter in his weakness, deny having known Me. Still, I wait for them to turn to Me. My Face is, at every moment, turned towards them. I will give them light to return to Me. I wait for them in the Sacrament of My Love.

(*In Sinu Iesu-When Heart Speaks to Heart -The Journal of a Priest*)

Adore and visit Jesus, abandoned and forsaken by men in His Sacrament of Love. Man has time for everything except for visits to His Lord and God, Who is waiting and longing for us in the Blessed Sacrament. The streets and places of entertainment are filled with people; the House of God is deserted. Men flee from it; they are afraid of it. Ah! Poor Jesus! Did you expect so much indifference from those You have redeemed, from Your friends, from Your children, from me?

Sympathize with Jesus Who is betrayed, insulted, mocked, and crucified far more ignominiously in His Sacrament of Love than He was in the Garden of Olives, in Jerusalem, and on Calvary. Those whom He has the most honored, loved, and enriched with His gifts and graces are the very ones who offend Him the most by their indifference.

(Saint Peter Julian Eymard)

Neither theological knowledge nor social action alone is enough to keep us in love with Christ unless both are proceeded by a personal encounter with Him. Theological insights are gained not only from between two covers of a book, but from two bent knees before an altar. The Holy Hour becomes like an oxygen tank to revive the breath of the Holy Spirit in the midst of the foul and fetid atmosphere of the world.

(Venerable Fulton J. Sheen)

And if you and I love our faulty fellow-human beings, how much more must God love us all? If we as human parents, can forgive our children any neglect, any crime, and work and pray patiently to make them better, how much more does God love us?

You may say perhaps: 'How do we know He does, if there is a He!' And I can only answer that we know it because He is here present with us today in the Blessed Sacrament on the altar, that He never has left us, and that by daily going to Him for the gift of Himself as daily bread, I am convinced of that love. I have the Faith that feeding at that table has nourished my soul so that there is life in it, and a lively realization that there is such a thing as the love of Christ for us.

It took me a long time as a convert to realize the presence of Christ as Man in the Sacrament. He is the same Jesus Who walked on earth, Who slept in the boat as the tempest arose, Who hungered in the desert, Who prayed in the garden, Who conversed with the woman by the well, Who rested at the house of Martha and Mary, Who wandered through the cornfields, picking the ears of corn to eat. Jesus is there as Man. He is there, Flesh and Blood, Soul and Divinity. He is our leader Who is always with us. Do you wonder that Catholics are exultant in this knowledge, that their Leader is with them? 'I am with you all days, even to the consummation of the world'.

(*Another Letter to an Agnostic* - Dorothy Day, The Catholic Worker, September 1, 1934.)

I desire to unite Myself to human souls; My great delight is to unite Myself with souls. Know, my daughter, that when I come to a human heart in Holy Communion, My hands are full of all kinds of graces which I want to give to the soul. But souls do not even pay attention to Me; they leave Me to myself and busy themselves with other things. Oh, how sad I am that souls do not recognize Love! They treat me as a dead object.

(Jesus to Saint Maria Faustina Kowalska)

Ah, how it hurts to see in what manner our Savior is treated! There He is in the tabernacle, the Prisoner of Love, waiting for souls to come and visit Him. But whoever gives Him even a thought, one only thought? ...It would cause so very little trouble to go to Him...for just a sweet moment. It would be so very easy to cast a tender glance upon that tiny door...to send a loving thought a-speeding towards that tabernacle...to breathe a few whispered words of affection...but, alas! When it comes to doing something for Jesus that something, no matter how small, becomes at once irksome and grievous-so weak are we!

(*Eucharistic Whisperings* - Father Winfrid Herbst, S.D.S.)

Why did Jesus not limit His Eucharistic Presence to the solemn moments of Holy Mass? Why does He not continue it only during those hours when, amid lights and flowers, He receives the adoration and homage of His sons? Why does He remain also during the nights, even in tabernacles where He is abandoned and forgotten and sometimes subjected to sacrilegious profanation?

It would seem that this persistent miracle of the Real Presence of Jesus under the appearances of the consecrated bread, even in times of profanation, is an excessive prodigality, both useless and incompatible with the Divine Majesty.

And yet, this is the very reason why Jesus chose to do so; to love with a love that knows no measure and does not shrink from excess. This was the purpose for which He invented and instituted the Holy Eucharist as we have it. 'He loved to the end'.

(*The Holy Eucharist* - Jose Guadalupe Trevino)

O inestimable charity! Even as You, true God and true Man, gave Yourself entirely to us, so also You left Yourself entirely for us, to be our food, so that during our earthly pilgrimage we would not faint with weariness, but would be strengthened by You, our celestial Bread. O man, what has your God left you? He has left you Himself, wholly God and wholly Man, concealed under the whiteness of bread. O fire of love! Was it not enough for You to have created us to Your image and likeness, and to have recreated us in grace through the Blood of Your Son, without giving Yourself wholly to us as our Food, O God, Divine Essence? What impelled You to do this? Your charity alone. It was not enough for You to send Your Word to us for our redemption; neither were You content to give Him us as our Food, but in the excess of Your love for Your creature, You gave to man the whole Divine essence . . .

(Saint Catherine of Siena)

If souls but understood the Treasure they possess in the Divine Eucharist, it would be necessary to encircle the tabernacles with the strongest ramparts for, in the delirium of a devouring and holy hunger, they would press forward themselves to feed on the Bread of Angels. The Churches would overflow with adorers consumed with love for the Divine Prisoner no less by night than by day.

(Blessed Dina Belanger)

It has been said, and rightly so, that between contemplation and adoration there is so close a union, so mutual a relationship, that they cannot be separated. We adore while contemplating and we contemplate while adoring. The saints in heaven live in perpetual adoration, because their joy is derived from eternal contemplation. On earth, where in some manner we must imitate the life of heaven, Christian devotion has striven to make the Sacred Host the center of perpetual contemplation and adoration, as far as human frailty permits. And both adoration and contemplation have called for perpetual exposition of the Blessed Sacrament.

The Sacred Host perpetually exposed on its Eucharistic throne, and, before it, day and night, loving souls in adoration and contemplation! Is this not truly heaven on earth?

(The Holy Eucharist - Jose Guadalupe Trevino)

My child, if My True Presence on the altar were limited to one place alone, many people from all parts of the world would try to visit that place at some time or other in their lives. Yet, now, that I have made it easy for all to come to Me, see how many visit Me only when they are obliged!

Many people are so cold toward me. Like children they are impressed only by what they can touch and see. I have given them the greatest Treasure in the Blessed Sacrament. Through My Apostles and their successors, I have promised to be personally present wherever the Blessed Sacrament is. Make every effort to be deeply impressed by this greatest of all earthly gifts.

It is not enough for you to believe in My Real Presence upon the altar. I placed Myself there for love of you. I wanted to be near you in some visible way, so that you might visit Me as often as you wished. You should wish it as often as possible.

(My Daily Bread - Father Anthony J. Paone, S.J.)

Lay the tired brain, the strained muscles, the aching head –
lay them all down at His feet without a word, just for His eye
to rest on and His Heart to help and heal.

(*Coram Sanctissimo* - Mother Mary Loyola)

If I personally fail to honor Our Lord in the Blessed
Sacrament, He will not remain without honor there. Other
faithful Catholics will give Him the honor that is due to His
presence and so compensate to some extent for my
negligence. But if I fail to honor the Son of God as He is
present with the Father and Holy Spirit in the tabernacle of
my own heart, no man can compensate for my indifference.
The inner sanctuary of my own heart is utterly and eternally
inaccessible to any except myself and God. If I am in the
state of grace, God is really present there in most profound
silence and solitude. None but myself can hope to penetrate
into that inmost sanctuary to do Him honor and hold
converse with Him. It is quite possible that in fact I have
never penetrated there. There are many people — dare we say
most people? — who have never withdrawn themselves from
the distractions of the senses to enter into that sacred shrine
of the soul where they can be alone with God. Yet without
devotion to the real presence of God within our souls there
can be no full development of our spiritual life, which is
essentially an interior life. 'Let it be plainly understood that
we cannot return to God unless we first enter into ourselves.
God is everywhere, but not everywhere to us. There is but
one point in the universe where God communicates with us,
and that is the center of our own soul. There He waits for us;
there He meets us; there He speaks to us. To seek Him,
therefore, we must enter into our own interior' (Archbishop
Ullathorne).

(*The Presence of God* - Father Anselm Moynihan, O.P.)

...Mary continues to stand alongside her Redeemer-Son in the Sacrament of the altar. It is consoling to recall that she who bears the title 'Mother of Fair Hope' keeps perpetual vigil before the Blessed Sacrament, ever ready to encourage her pilgrim children enroute to the glorious world of the resurrection. In the *Salve Regina* we 'poor banished children of Eve' hail the New Eve, mother of the Eucharist, as 'our life, our sweetness and our hope.' And we implore her to 'show us, after this exile, the blessed fruit' of her womb.

This our heavenly mother will certainly do, lovingly and graciously. But already here and now, that is, during our exile in this 'vale of tears,' she untiringly shows us the blessed fruit of her womb integrally present in the Sacrament of the altar. As His handmaid and herald, she urges us to draw ever closer to Him. For not only is He the source of life and holiness; He is the pledge and pattern of our bodily resurrection when the new world finally dawns.

(*Mary and the Eucharist* - Father Richard Foley, S.J.)

Oh, the wonderful and hidden grace of this Sacrament which only the faithful of Christ understand, which unbelievers and slaves of sin cannot experience! In it, spiritual grace is conferred, lost virtue restored, and the beauty, marred by sin, repaired. At times, indeed, its grace is so great that, from the fullness of the devotion, not only the mind but also the frail body feels filled with greater strength.

Nevertheless, our neglect and coldness are much to be deplored and pitied, when we are not moved to receive with greater fervor Christ in Whom is the hope and merit of all who will be saved. He is our sanctification and redemption.

He is our consolation in this life and the eternal joy of the blessed in heaven. This being true, it is lamentable that many pay so little heed to the salutary Mystery which fills the heavens with joy and maintains the whole universe in being.

Oh, the blindness and the hardness of the heart of man that does not show more regard for so wonderful a gift, but rather falls into carelessness from its daily use! If this most Holy Sacrament were celebrated in only one place and consecrated by only one priest in the whole world, with what great desire, do you think, would men be attracted to that place, to that priest of God, in order to witness the celebration of the Divine Mysteries!

(*The Imitation of Christ* - Thomas a Kempis)

There have been newly converted Christians, in the Indies and in Japan, who have traveled more than a hundred leagues every year, to have the consolation of once adoring Jesus Christ in the most Blessed Sacrament, of hearing one single Mass; and they thought nothing of the fatigue, of so difficult a journey, that they might have the happiness of spending half an hour with Jesus Christ.

My God! How many will rise up at the day of judgment and will condemn us! We have Jesus Christ in our town; religious persons have Jesus Christ in their own house; and this benefit is esteemed as nothing! And some value it so little, that they only visit Jesus Christ with indifference and even with repugnance, and almost all without devotion.

(*Devotion to The Sacred Heart* - Father John Croiset, S.J.)

[CHRIST]:...Here upon the altar you will find not a relic, nor a monument to someone's memory, but Me, alive as ever, all-powerful, all-loving, all-perfect. All the treasures and wonders of this world – these things are nothing compared to what you find upon the altar. You will not be drawn to Me by any curiosity or shallow virtue. Only a firm faith, a steady hope, and a burning love will draw you to Me and keep you loyal to Me.

Consider how great must be the tepidity and negligence of this world, since so many fail to take advantage of My gift of Holy Communion. It is sad to see how few are drawn to Me with tender affection and wordless gratitude. In this Sacrament, I offer Myself, in Whom lie all human hopes and merits for salvation.

(*How to Get More Out of Holy Communion* - Saint Peter Julian Eymard)

...the Sacramental Savior...abides on every altar as the Author and Finisher of our sanctification. We behold Him there no longer bruised and battered for our sins; no longer is there any visible evidence of the untold mental anguish, the agonizing physical pain, or the bitter desolation which He underwent to redeem us. But in the Holy Eucharist, He is the object of man's indifference and neglect. Although He conquered sin by His death and Resurrection, He is still within the range of the sinner's power to insult and outrage Him...

Great then and urgent is the need of reparation on our part for the pain of which the Eucharistic King is the daily silent Victim. Calm and restful though our gratitude may be in our moments of adoration, we must never forget the studied neglect, the worldliness of His wayward children, but rather strive persistently with all our powers to comfort Him in His Sacramental lowliness, while the storm of sin set in motion by the thoughtlessness, if not the malice, of so many, beats Him as ruthlessly and heartlessly as the steel scourge fell upon His virginal flesh and numbered all His bones.

(*Transforming Your Life Through the Eucharist* - Father John A. Kane)

The principal sorrow which afflicted the heart of Jesus so much was not the sight of the torments and infamy which men were preparing for Him, but the sight of their ingratitude towards His immense love. He distinctly foresaw all the sins which we should commit after all His sufferings and such a bitter and ignominious death. He foresaw, especially, the horrible insults which men would offer to His adorable heart, which He has left us in the Most Holy Sacrament as a proof of His affection. O my God, what affronts has not Jesus Christ received from men in this Sacrament of love?

(Saint Alphonsus Liguori)

Why art Thou left alone in this Most Holy Sacrament? Where are Thy adorers and Thy friends? Has Thy Church failed to announce Thy Gospel to the world, and to make Thy presence known? Why art Thou so ignored, forsaken, and left alone in Thy tabernacles, without honor and with no one to thank Thee for the gift of Thy Real Presence? Why is the world kept in the dark concerning Thee in this Most Holy Sacrament, when Thou art all that this world needs, and all that souls desire?

(*Vultus Christi - Thursday of Adoration and Reparation for Priests*)

Of ourselves, we cannot communicate worthily. We need the help of the Holy Spirit. Even though we approach the altar free from mortal sin, He must sharpen our spiritual apprehension and inflame our love to intense ardor, that Christ may find in us a more beautiful habitation every time we receive Him.

The Sacramental God has a divine right to expect on our part after each Holy Communion an intensification of our gradual growth into His likeness. As often as we receive Him, He would have us burn with the desire for greater progress in virtue that will manifest itself in an irrevocable detachment from the world and a more unselfish love of Him, grounded on the conviction of our nothingness and consequent sore need of Him.

With greater joy will He abide in us if He beholds us by degrees assimilating His life, resembling Him in virtue by more complete conformity to His will. Christ will unite Himself most intimately with us if we are constant in our effort to imitate Him.

(Transforming Your Life Through the Eucharist - Father John A. Kane)

If you would become all that God intended you to be, if you would have life and success in life, if you would have love and not love's base counterfeit, you will enter into a union with God as intimate and as vital as that which exists between a mother and the babe in her womb; in very brief, you will cling to Jesus Christ in Holy Communion! He is your only hope for success, your only means to sanctification, your one true life and real love. Cling to Him...

(A Trappist Asks Do You Want Life and Love?)

Help me dear Lord, to address You with the same love and confidence as if I really saw You. I know that all my concerns, spiritual and temporal, are of deepest interest to Your loving Heart; and that You are willing and anxious to help and to console me. There is no cross so great that I should not feel relief after speaking of it to You, no annoyance too trivial to be unworthy of Your sympathy. How many difficulties would be cleared away, how many unkind and angry thoughts would vanish, how much slighter my daily troubles and worries would appear, if I would only come and tell You of them.

Give me, then, Lord, this ardent faith and loving confidence. As Saint John, with love-quickened eyes, recognized You through the dim mists of the dawn on the shores of the lake, so may my heart, each time I enter Your Sacred Presence, echo his cry of joy: 'It is the Lord.' Thus will Your sanctuary become for me a haven of rest and consolation, where I may gain strength to continue my journey; until the dawn of that happy day, when, purified and sanctified by Your sufferings and merits, I shall joyfully enter Your heavenly kingdom, there to behold forever Your unveiled glory. Amen.

(An Hour with Our Savior)

Consider how devoted My saints were to Me. They seized every opportunity to visit Me and stay with Me. They desired to abandon all useless interests so that they might have more time with Me. In return for this generosity with Me, they received a clearer understanding of My boundless goodness and a deeper appreciation of My infinite love.

You too have the opportunity to give Me more of your time and attention. Make a greater effort to come closer to Me in friendship. You have the privilege of kneeling before Me like the simple, wonderful shepherds; the tired, admiring Magi; the suffering, begging leper; the penitent, hopeful Magdalene, the convinced, converted Thomas. How are you taking advantage of this privilege?

How much easier it will be for you to face Me in your judgment if you have loved to face Me often during your earthly life. Each visit to Me is an act of faith, of love, and of self-purification. Come to Me often, so that I may shower more of My gifts upon your soul.

(*My Daily Bread* - Father Anthony J. Paone, S.J.)

If a list of priorities were drawn up for a given parish, or a given diocese, where would Eucharistic Adoration be on that list? How much time, energy, and concentration would be devoted in establishing perpetual adoration in each parish? In his first encyclical letter, *Redemptor Hominis,* Pope John Paul II exhorted that 'every member of the Church, especially bishops and priests, must be vigilant in seeing that this Sacrament of love shall be at the center of the life of the people of God, so that through all the manifestations of wor-ship due to it, Christ shall be given back love for love; and truly become the life of our souls.'

Let us remember, that the Sacred Heart of Jesus in the Blessed Sacrament has still, as far as can be, the same sentiments It always had. It is always inflamed with love for man, always sensibly touched by our misfortunes, always urged by the desire to make us partakers of Its treasures and to give Itself to us, always disposed to receive us, and to serve as a dwelling and a paradise for us, even in this life, and above all, as a refuge at the hour of death.

And, for all this, what sentiments of gratitude does He find in the hearts of men? What solicitude? What love? He loves, and He is not loved. We do not even know His love, because we do not condescend to receive the gifts by which He would show it to us, nor listen to the tender and secret declarations that He would make of it to our hearts. Is not this a motive powerful enough to touch the hearts of all who are at all reasonable, and who have some little tenderness for Jesus Christ?

Our loving Savior, in instituting this Sacrament of love, foresaw clearly all the ingratitude of mankind. He felt by anticipation in His Sacred Heart, all the grief which it was to cause Him. Yet all this could not keep Him at a distance, nor prevent Him from showing us the excess of His love, in the institution of this adorable mystery.

(Devotion to The Sacred Heart - Father John Croiset, S.J.)

He stated that 'indeed, the Eucharist is the ineffable Sacrament! The essential commitment and, above all, the visible grace and source of supernatural strength for the Church as the people of God is to persevere and advance constantly in Eucharistic life and Eucharistic piety and to develop spiritually in the climate of the Eucharist. With all the greater reason, then, it is not permissible for us, in thought, life, or action, to take away from this truly most Holy Sacrament its full magnitude and its essential meaning. It is at one and the same time a Sacrifice - Sacrament, a Communion-Sacrament, and a Presence-Sacrament.'

(Come to Me in the Blessed Sacrament)

If only souls knew the power to purify and to transform that emanates from My tabernacles!

If only My priests knew this they would hasten into My presence and remain there, waiting for Me to do in them what, of themselves, they cannot do.

(In Sinu Jesu – When Heart Speaks to Heart - The Journal of a Priest)

[It's not that difficult to be a good Catholic.] There is no gimmick. We just (1) believe everything God has told us through Church and Scripture, and (2) respond with adoration.

And then everything else that is necessary will follow – as it did for Mary, for whom there was 'only one thing needful,' and as it did for all the saints, and as it does for Mother Teresa's Missionaries of Charity, who are simply the holiest and happiest people in this entire world.

Adoration means especially Eucharistic Adoration. In that silence, there is power greater than a thousand nuclear weapons, greater than the sun, greater than the Big Bang. It is the power of God released when the atom of the Trinity was split on the Cross and the explosion of redeeming blood came out. In Eucharistic Adoration we touch this power, which is the root of everything, for it is Christ the Pantocrator (i.e. ruler of the universe, creator and savior). We touch the candle of our souls to the fire of His passion, His passion for souls, and we catch the flame.

(Jesus Shock - Peter Kreeft, Ph.D.)

You can feel Him...Oh yes, here you can feel God... you can inhale and breathe Him, filling this humble cenacle of the earth, impregnating the atmosphere with celestial perfume. This tabernacle bears the fragrance of Jesus; one enters here as if entering Jesus' innermost being; with that same respect...that same confidence...that same love. The light, the warmth, the fire of the Eucharistic Jesus fills everything, and thus, in this beloved enclosure, the thorns are roses...sacrifice is not felt...pain and martyrdom are sweet because they are suffered for His sake and in His intimacy.

If the altar is poor, Jesus is its richness...its most delicate embellishment. Without being fully aware of it, one enters into profound concentration and prayer because one leaves earthly things at the door, and the soul is engulfed in the possession of its Beloved.

Here - all alone, He and I — He, with all His greatness, and I with all my miseries — He, all fire; and I, burning in the midst of His Divine Passion!...My darkness is lost in the midst of His light...and my icy heart melts inside of His. Here my sins are forgiven and my sorrows — - O! my sorrows are united to His own, giving them value...How many treasures are enclosed in this holy place, consecrated through the presence of Jesus in the Blessed Sacrament! Heaven is here, because He is here!

I would not exchange these four walls for the most glorious palace on earth! You can feel Him, yes... here the Lord can be felt...here He can be found...here the soul loses itself in His arms. It cries out contritely, is anxious to suffer, and loves Him!

(*Holy Hours* - Concepcion Carbrera de Armida)

I told Him this morning in Holy Communion that I want to belong wholly to Him and that always...What a loving glance He gave me then! O how far away from Him my thoughts already are...how far away my heart...how far!

O why do I treat Him so? Poor Jesus! He always thinks of me, and I think so seldom of Him.

(*Eucharistic Whisperings* - Father Winfrid Herbst, S.D.S.)

Day after day we foolishly seek affirmation, comfort, contentment, and fulfillment in people and things that are powerless to satiate our ingrained desire to be happy and at peace. There is only One Source of happiness in this world - Jesus Christ, who offers Himself to us every day.

Tragic, isn't it, that so many of us, decline His invitation to physical and spiritual intimacy. And we wonder why there is so much unhappiness in this world.

Jesus Christ during his life on earth, never passed by anywhere without pouring out His abundant blessings, from which we can deduce how great and precious must be the gifts which those who have the happiness of receiving Him in Holy Communion must share or rather, that all the happiness we can have in this life consists in receiving our Lord in Holy Communion.

(Saint John Vianney)

Run to the Feet of Jesus!

We must always have courage, and if some spiritual languor comes upon us, let us run to the feet of Jesus in the Blessed

Sacrament, and let us place ourselves in the midst of the heavenly perfumes, and we will undoubtedly regain our strength.

Kneel down and render the tribute of your presence and devotion to Jesus in the Blessed Sacrament. Confide all your needs to Him, along with those of others. Speak to Him with filial abandonment, give free rein to your heart, and give Him complete freedom to work in you as He thinks best.

(Saint Pio of Pietrelcina)

Jesus Christ true God and true Man! My soul rejoices to find You in the Blessed Sacrament, You the uncreated God who became man, a creature! In this Sacrament, O Christ, I find both Your humanity and Your Divinity; from Your humanity I rise to Your Divinity; and from it I go back to Your humanity.

I see Your ineffable Divinity which contains all the treasures of wisdom, of knowledge, of incorruptible riches. I see the inexhaustible fountain of delights which alone can satisfy our intelligence. I see Your most precious soul, O Jesus, with all the virtues and gifts of the Holy Spirit, a holy and unspotted oblation; I see Your Sacred Body, the price of our redemption; I see Your Blood, which purifies and vivifies us; in brief, I find treasures which are so precious and so great that I cannot comprehend them.

(*Divine Intimacy: Meditations on the Interior Life for Every Day of the Liturgical Year.* - Father Gabriel of Saint Mary Magdalen, O.C.D., quoting Saint Angela of Foligno)

We go to see Jesus hidden in the tabernacle. All distance is annihilated and even time loses its boundaries before this Presence which is eternal life, the seed of Resurrection and a foretaste of heavenly bliss. It is from here that a Christian's life radiates forth Christ's life; in the midst of his work, in his habitual smile, in the way he accepts setbacks and pains, the Christian reflects Christ. He who remains for us in the tabernacle manifests Himself to men and makes Himself present in them in the everyday life of a Christian. Tabernacles of silver and gold that give shelter to the omnipresence of Jesus, our treasure, our life, our knowledge, I bless and adore the One who inhabits you with profound reverence.

(*Sow!* - Sister Cristina de Artega)

...You see that same Body, not in a manger, but upon the altar; not carried in His Mother's arms, but elevated in the priest's hands. Let us, therefore, be roused, and tremble, and bring with us more devotion to the altar than those Eastern kings did to the manger, where they adored their newborn Savior.

(Saint John Chrysostom)

When we go to Holy Communion, all of us receive the same Lord Jesus, but not all receive the same grace nor are the same effects produced in all. This comes from our greater or lesser disposition. To explain this fact, I will take an example from nature. Consider the process of grafting, the more similar the one plant is to the other, the better the graft will succeed. Likewise, the more resemblance there is between the one that goes to Communion and Jesus, so much the better will the fruits of Holy Communion be.

(*Jesus Our Eucharistic Lord* – Stefano M. Manelli, quoting Saint Anthony Mary Claret)

Jesus Christ finds the means to console a soul that remains with a recollected spirit before the Most Blessed Sacrament, far beyond what the world can do with all its feasts and pastimes. Oh, how sweet a joy it is to remain with faith and tender devotion before an altar, and converse familiarly with Jesus Christ, who is there for the express purpose of listening to and graciously hearing those who pray to Him; to ask His pardon for the displeasures which we have caused Him; to represent our wants to Him, as a friend does to a friend in whom he places all his confidence; to ask Him for His graces, for His love, and for His kingdom; but above all, oh, what a heaven it is there to remain making acts of love towards that Lord who is on the very altar praying to the Eternal Father for us, and is there burning with love for us. Indeed, that love it is which detains Him there, thus hidden and unknown, and where He is even despised by ungrateful souls! But why should we say more? 'Taste and see'.

(*Visits to the Most Blessed Sacrament and the Blessed Virgin Mary* - Saint Alphonsus Liquori)

Is it not just, amidst so much incredulity and coldness, so many profanations and outrages, that this God of love should find at least some friends of His Sacred Heart, who should be pained by the little love felt for Him, feel the injuries offered Him, be faithful and assiduous in adoring Him in the Holy Eucharist, and neglect nothing in order to repair, by their love, by their adorations, and by every kind of homage, all the outrages to which the excess of His love daily exposes Him, in this august Sacrament?

(*Devotion to the Sacred Heart* - Father John Croiset, S.J.)

Dear Eucharistic soul: In that hour [of the Last Supper] Jesus thought of you. Have no doubt about it. He thought of you in particular, and had you before His eyes. He understood that, without that small, white, consecrated wafer, which you adore and which you receive every morning, you would feel lonely, very lonely, in your exile here below. He knew that your heart would hunger and thirst for love and be the prey of unmitigated nostalgia for heaven. He knew that on the road through life you would find many a cause for grief and, behind a smiling appearance, would have to conceal many a galling sorrow. And for your sake, dear soul, lest you be orphaned and without a loyal friend in whose understanding heart you might pour out the overflowing bitterness of your heart, Jesus overlooked all those sacrileges, profanations, and ingratitudes and, in that night, instituted the Eucharist for you — understand this well! — just for you. And for your sake He has remained in that small, white, consecrated Host which you receive each morning. Do you understand now, dear soul, how much you are loved by the Christ of the Cenacle and of the Eucharist?

(*The Holy Eucharist* - Jose Guadalupe Trevino)

Jesus, my God, I adore You, here present in the Blessed Sacrament of the altar, where You wait day and night to be our comfort while we await Your unveiled presence in heaven. Jesus, my God, I adore You in all places where the Blessed Sacrament is reserved and where sins are committed against this Sacrament of Love. Jesus, my God, I adore You for all time, past, present and future, for every soul that ever was, is or shall be created. Jesus, my God, who for us has endured hunger and cold, labor and fatigue, I adore You.

Jesus, my God, who for my sake has deigned to subject Yourself to the humiliation of temptation, to the perfidy and defection of friends, to the scorn of Your enemies, I adore You. Jesus, my God, who for us has endured the buffeting of Your passion, the scourging, the crowning with thorns, the heavy weight of the cross, I adore You. Jesus, my God, who, for my salvation and that of all mankind, was cruelly nailed to the cross and hung there for three long hours in bitter agony, I adore You. Jesus, my God, who for love of us did institute this Blessed Sacrament and offer Yourself daily for the sins of men, I adore You. Jesus, my God, who in Holy Communion became the food of my soul, I adore You. 'Jesus, for You I live. Jesus, for You I die. Jesus, I am Yours in life and death'.

(*Reflections and Prayers for Visits with our Eucharistic Lord* - John J. Cardinal Carberry)

After uttering the words which bring Christ down upon the altar, look at the Sacramental Species with the eyes of faith.

As you kneel, see the legions of angels which surround Christ and adore Him with profound reverence. This sight should make you exceedingly humble.

In the elevation, contemplate Christ elevated on the Cross. Ask Him to bring all things to Himself. Make fervent acts of faith, hope, love, adoration, humility, saying with the mind, 'Jesus, Son of God, have mercy on me! My Lord and my God I love you, my God I adore you with my whole heart and soul'. You may also renew the intention of the Mass which you are celebrating, offering up the Eucharist according to its four ends.

But when you lift up the chalice, make sure to remember in a very contrite way that the blood of Christ has been shed for you, even though you have oftentimes despised it. Adore Him so as to make up for your past neglect.

(*The Sacrifice of the Mass* - Cardinal Giovanni Bona)

Moreover, you must console our Lord. He expects consolation from you and will receive it with pleasure. Ask Him to prepare good priests for Himself; priests who are apostolic and zealous for the salvation of souls; priests who are the glory of their age and who present God with kingdoms. Beg Him to take ownership of everything, and to be not only a Savior - that supposes nothing but sacrifice - but a King, and a King of peace with absolute power. Console Him for His being so little treated as a King in His own kingdom. Alas! Our Lord is vanquished! In heaven, He is an all-powerful Ruler Who commands saints and angels and is faithfully obeyed. Not so here below. Men, - the children He ransomed - have got the best of Him. He no longer rules over Catholic peoples. Let us establish His kingdom in us at least, and work at restoring it everywhere.

(*New Year Wishes to Our Eucharistic Lord* - Saint Peter Julian Eymard)

The holy hour in our modern rat race is necessary for authentic prayer. Our world is one of speed in which intensity of movement is a substitute for lack of purpose; where noise is invoked to drown out the whisperings of conscience; where talk, talk, talk gives the impression that we are doing something when really we are not; where activity kills self-knowledge won by contemplation...

There seems to be so little in common between our involvement with the news of the world and the Stranger in whose Presence we find ourselves. The hour means giving up a golf game or a cocktail party, or a nap…

Sometimes it is hard, especially during vacation when we have nothing to do. I remember once having two hours between trains in Paris. I went to the Church of Saint Roch to make my holy hour. There are not ten days a year I can sleep in the daytime. This was one. I was so tired, I sat down at 2:00 p.m. - too tired to kneel - and went to sleep. I slept perfectly until 3:00 p.m. I said to the Good Lord: 'Did I make a holy hour?' The answer came back: 'Yes! That's the way the Apostles made their first one.' The best time to make a holy hour is in the morning, early, before the day sets traps for us. By being faithful to it, and letting nothing interfere with it, we use it as the sign and symbol of our victimhood. We are not called to great penances, and many would interfere with our duty, but the hour is our daily sacrifice in union with Christ.

(Venerable Fulton J. Sheen)

Listen. Jesus is speaking…Being in heaven I came down to earth; and then I instituted the Blessed Sacrament in order to be with you always. In Holy Communion I really and truly come to you…And you?…When do you come to Me? In Holy Communion I visit you; but, tell Me, My child, when do you visit Me? Perhaps our Sacred meeting in the morning satisfies you; it does not satisfy Me. I long to see you here in My presence again before evening. My child. That is why I now invite you. Won't you accept the invitation?

(*Eucharistic Whisperings* - Father Winfrid Herbst, S.D.S.)

Like Mary, let us be full of zeal to go in haste to give Jesus to others. She was full of grace when, at the annunciation, she received Jesus. Like her, we too become full of grace every time we receive Holy Communion. It is the same Jesus whom she received and whom we receive at Mass. As soon as she received Him she went with haste to give Him to John. For us also, as soon as we receive Jesus in Holy Communion, let us go in haste to give Him to our sisters, to our poor, to the sick, to the dying, to the lepers, to the unwanted, and the unloved. By this we make Jesus present in the world today.

(Attributed to Saint Teresa of Calcutta)

The devotion to the Blessed Eucharist and the devotion to the Sacred Heart are not only two sister devotions, in reality, they are only one and the same devotion. They complete each other and develop each other; they blend so perfectly together that one cannot stand without the other, and their union is absolute. Not only can one of these devotions not be prejudicial to the other but, because they complete each other and perfect each other, they also reciprocally increase each other.

If we have devotion to the Sacred Heart, we will wish to find It, to adore It, to love It, to offer It our reparation and praise, and where shall we look for It but in the Blessed Eucharist where It is found eternally living?

If we love this adorable Heart, we will wish to unite ourselves to It, for love seeks union, we will wish to warm our hearts by the ardor of this divine fire, but to reach the Sacred Heart, to take hold of It, to put It in contact with our own, what shall we do? Shall we scale heaven to bear away the Heart of Jesus Who reigns triumphant in glory? There is no need to do so. We will go to the Blessed Eucharist, we will go to the tabernacle, we will take the white Host, and when we have enclosed it in our breast, we will feel the divine Heart truly beating beside our own.

(*The Book of Infinite Love* - Mother Louise Margaret Claret)

The coming of Jesus at Bethlehem brought joy to the world and to every human heart. The same Jesus comes again and again in our hearts during Holy Communion. He wants to give the same joy and peace....

Every time I hear anyone speak of the Sacred Heart of Jesus or of the Blessed Sacrament I feel an indescribable joy. It is as if a wave of precious memories, sweet affections and joyful hopes swept over my poor person, making me tremble with happiness and filling my soul with tenderness. These are loving appeals from Jesus who wants me wholeheartedly there, at the source of all goodness, His Sacred Heart, throbbing mysteriously behind the Eucharistic veils...I love to repeat today 'Sweet Heart of my Jesus, make me love You more and more.'

(*Journal of a Soul* - Saint John XXIII)

Put your sins in the chalice for the Precious Blood to wash away. One drop is capable of washing away all the sins of the world.

(Attributed to Saint Teresa of Calcutta)

The Heart of Jesus therefore lives in the Eucharist, since His body is alive there. It is true that we can neither feel nor see that Divine Heart, but things are pretty much the same for all men. This principle of life must be mysterious and veiled; to uncover it would kill it. We can conclude to its existence only from the effects it produces. A man does not ask to see the heart of a dear friend; one word is enough to tell him of his love. But how will the Divine Heart of Jesus make Itself known? It manifests Itself to us by the sentiments with which It inspires us; that should suffice. Besides, who could contemplate the beauty and the goodness of the Divine Heart? Who could stand the brightness of its glory, the consuming and devouring flames of this fire of love? Who would dare look at this divine Ark, on which is written Its gospel of love in letters which Its love has its throne, and Its goodness all Its treasures? Who would want to penetrate into the very sanctuary of the Godhead? The Heart of Jesus! Why, it is the heaven of heavens, in which God Himself dwells and finds His delights!

No! We do not see the Eucharistic Heart of Jesus! But we possess It; It is ours!

(*Reflections on the Sacred Heart of Jesus in the Most Blessed Sacrament -* Saint Peter Julian Eymard)

It is for us that, during eighteen [now twenty] hundred years, our Divine Savior has remained day and night on our altars, that we may have recourse to Him in all our needs; and nothing so much afflicts His Divine Heart as our ingratitude for such a favor, and our neglect to visit Him and ask His blessing. If we knew how profitable those visits are, we should be constantly prostrate before the altar. The Saints understood this truth; they knew that Jesus Christ is the source of all grace, and whenever they encountered any difficulty or wished to obtain any particular favor, they ran to

Jesus Christ in the Blessed Sacrament. Saint Francis Xavier, Saint Francis Regis and others spent whole hours during the day and, frequently, a great part of the night at the foot of the altar; it was in these long interviews with Jesus Christ that they advanced the good works they had in hand, converted sinners, and obtained success in all their undertakings for the glory of God and their own sanctification.

(Saint J. B. Marcellin Champagnat)

Above all, do not allow - as some do, who are deceived under the pretext of restoring the liturgy or who idly claim that only liturgical rites are of any real value and dignity - that churches be closed during the hours not appointed for public functions, as has already happened in some places: where the adoration of the august Sacrament and visits to our Lord in the tabernacles are neglected; where confession or devotion is discouraged; and devotion to the Virgin Mother of God, a sign of 'predestination' according to the opinion of holy men, is so neglected, especially among the young, as to fade away and gradually vanish. Such conduct most harmful to Christian piety is like poisonous fruit, growing on the infected branches of a healthy tree, which must be cut off so that the life-giving sap of the tree may bring forth only the best fruit.

(*Mediator Dei* – Venerable Pope Pius XII)

Devotion to the Sacred Heart should bring us to a life of intimate union with Jesus who, we know, is truly present and living in the Eucharist. The two devotions — to the Sacred Heart and to the Eucharist — are closely connected. They call upon one another and, we may even say, they require one another. The Sacred Heart explains the mystery of the love of Jesus by which He becomes bread in order to nourish us with His substance, while in the Eucharist we have the Real Presence of this same Heart, living in our midst.

It is wonderful to contemplate Jesus as the symbol of His infinite love, but it is even more wonderful to find Him always near us in the Sacrament of the altar. The Sacred Heart which we honor is not a dead person's heart which no longer palpitates, so that we have only the memory of him, but it is the Heart of a living Person, of One who lives eternally. He lives not only in heaven where His Sacred humanity dwells in glory, but He lives also on earth wherever the Eucharist is reserved.

In speaking of the Eucharist, Our Lord says to us, 'Behold, I am with you all days, even to the consummation of the world' (Mt 28, 20). In Holy Communion, then, this Heart beats within us, it touches our heart; through the love of this Heart, we are fed with His Flesh and with His Blood, so that we may abide in Him and He in us.

(*Divine Intimacy: Meditations on the Interior Life for Every Day of the Liturgical Year* - Father Gabriel of Saint Mary Magdalen, O.C.D.)

If the Blessed Sacrament is Jesus all for us, is it not the most legitimate of conclusions that we should be all for Him? We should be all for Jesus, if Jesus is our all. And what does this mean? Surely, among other things, that the Blessed Sacrament should be to us just the single overpowering fact of the world. Our hands hold Him; our words make Him; our tongue rests Him; our body compasses Him; our souls feel Him; our flesh feeds upon Him, the Infinite, the Incomprehensible, the Immense, the Eternal. Must not all life be looked at in this light, just as the whole Church lies in this light and has no other?

(*The Blessed Sacrament* - Father Frederick Faber)

Is there any real difference between Jesus in heaven and Jesus in the Eucharist? No, it is the same Jesus. The only difference is in us. We now on earth cannot see or touch Him with our senses. But that is not a limitation in Him; it is a limitation in us.

We speak correctly of believing in the Real Presence. But we should grow in our understanding of what this implies.

The living, breathing Jesus Christ is in the Blessed Sacrament. This is the reality. When we speak of presence, however, we are saying something more.

Two people may be really near each other physically, but not present to each other spiritually. To be present to someone means to have another person in mind by being mentally aware of their existence, and to have them in one's heart by loving that other person...

Jesus is on earth in the Blessed Sacrament. Why? In order that we might come to Him now no less than His contemporaries did in first century Palestine. If we thus approach Him in loving faith, there is no limit to the astounding things He will do. Why not? In the Eucharist, He has the same human lips that told the raging storm, 'Be still!' and commanded the dead man, 'Lazarus, come forth!'

There are no limitations to Christ's power, as God, which He exercises through His humanity in the Eucharist. The only limitation is our own weakness of faith or lack of confidence in His almighty love.

(*Soul Magazine* - Servant of God, Father John A. Hardon, S.J.)

Most adorable and most amiable Jesus! Ever full of love for us, ever touched with compassion for our miseries, ever actuated by the desire of making us partakers of Thy treasures, and of giving Thyself wholly to us: Jesus, my Savior and my God, Who, through an excess of the most ardent and most wonderful love, hast placed Thyself in the condition of a victim, in the Adorable Eucharist, where Thou offers Thyself for us in sacrifice so many times every day, what must be Thy sentiments in this state, at finding no return for all this, in the hearts of the greater part of men, but hardness, forgetfulness, ingratitude and contempt!

Was it not enough. Oh, my God, to have taken the most painful means of saving us, when Thou could have shown us Thy excessive love at much less cost? Was it not enough to abandon Thyself once to that cruel agony, and deadly sorrow, caused in Thee by the horrible sight of our sins, with which Thou was loaded?

Why would Thou still expose Thyself daily to all the insults of which the unspeakable malice of men and devils is capable? Ah! my God and my most loving Redeemer, what are the sentiments of Thy Sacred Heart at the sight of all this ingratitude, and of all these sins? How great was the bitterness with which so many sacrileges, and so many outrages, afflicted and tormented Thy Heart?…With a heart humbled and broken with grief, I ask of Thee a thousand and a thousand times pardon for all these indignities. Why cannot I, oh my God, wash with my blood every spot where Thy Sacred Heart has been so horribly outraged, and the greatest proof of Thy love received with such incredible contempt? …But oh, my beloved Savior, what covers me still more with confusion, and should fill me with greater grief is, that I also have been of the number of these ungrateful souls…

(*Devotion to the Sacred Heart* - Father John Croiset, S.J.)

We read in the Gospel of St John that when Jesus went to Bethany, to the house of his friend Lazarus, one of his friend's sisters, called Martha, busied herself about the house. The other, Mary, gave her entire attention to the Lord. It seems that this was by far the more commendable kind of action: if you receive a friend as a guest into your house, you look after him - that is, you keep him company and converse with him. You do not leave him in the sitting room, or anywhere else in the house reading the newspaper to amuse himself until you have time to attend to him. Without doubt this would be a dereliction of good manners. And if the person were of such importance that the mere fact of his coming to your house would be regarded as an honor far surpassing your condition and deserts, the discourtesy would be tantamount to a gross insult.

(*The Sacrifice of the Altar* - Federico Suarez)

How humbly Thou dost obey Thy priests! One word from their lips and Thou dost come down upon the altar in Holy Mass and renew the Sacrifice of Calvary in an unbloody manner. Thou dost permit Thy priests to give Thee as the Bread of Life to those who come to the Holy Table; Thou dost not shrink even from the unworthy. Thou dost allow Thyself to be carried wherever Thy priests bear Thee. Heaven and earth are subject to Thee, 0 King of Glory, and yet Thou dost lower Thyself before Thy sinful creatures, living with them in the Sacred Host - offering Thyself for them, coming to their hearts in Holy Communion.

(*A Novena of Holy Communions* - Father Lawrence G. Lovasik, SVD)

So long as we do not have a passionate love for our Lord in the Most Blessed Sacrament, we will have done nothing.

(Saint Peter Julian Eymard)

Like fire that transforms everything to itself, here in the Blessed Sacrament Jesus transforms everything to good in the fire of His Divine love, drawing good out of evil, drawing a greater good out of a greater evil, consuming even our very faults and failures - like straw thrown into a burning furnace - and using them to make us more humble and to bring us even closer to His Divine Heart...

It is never too late, and Jesus never gives up on anyone...

Our very weaknesses and failures endear us even more to the merciful love of His Eucharistic Heart...

No one loves us as Jesus loves us: with merciful love He loves us, not in spite of our sins, but because of our sins...

(*Rosary Meditations from Mother Teresa of Calcutta - Loving Jesus with The Heart of Mary*)

As He was physically formed in her, so He wills to be spiritually formed in you. If you knew He was seeing through your eyes, you would see in every fellowman a child of God. If you knew that He worked through your hands, they would bless all the day through. If you knew He spoke through your lips, then your speech, like Peter's, would betray that you had been with the Galilean. If you knew that He wants to use your mind, your will, your fingers, and your heart, how different you would be. If half the world did this there would be no war!

(*How to Find Christmas Peace* - Venerable Fulton J. Sheen)

I should never cease to express my sorrow for the neglect and coldness which is shown to Jesus in the Blessed Sacrament. How great must be His love for us, since He does not become disgusted with so much ingratitude. People go to the trouble to see various objects of beauty, curiosity, or entertainment. Yet, here upon the altar is the grandest, greatest, most magnificent of all beings. How dull can the human mind be! How hard can the human heart become! This is our all-loving Savior, our God! In Him we live, and move, and exist. Truly, without Him we are nothing. In Him alone shall I find perfect peace and all-satisfying happiness.

(*The Sacrifice of the Mass* - Cardinal Giovanni Bona)

It is in our churches, in this tabernacle, that the living body of the Savior rests. He was but nine months in the womb of Mary, three hours on the Cross, three days in the tomb. Yet He is always in our churches. This is why they do not empty of angels, archangels, and seraphim unceasingly adoring Him. They adore Him with signs of respect, with prostrations that, if we could perceive them, would strangely confound us. Our churches, if we might speak in such a way, are like an annex of paradise; there the Creator is adored, there the resurrected Savior finds a body and a soul, thereto the heavenly spirits journey, and there they delight in the same happiness savored beyond the firmament.

(*Christian Reflections* - Saint Claude de la Colombiere)

The Eucharist is the invention of Love! . . .Yet how few souls correspond to that love which spends and consumes itself for them! I live in the midst of sinners that I may be their life, their physician, and the remedy of the diseases bred by corrupt nature. And in return they forsake, insult, and despise Me.

...Poor pitiable sinners, do not turn away from me...Day and night, I am on the watch for you in the tabernacle. I will not reproach you...I will not cast your sins in your face...

But I will wash them in My Blood and in My Wounds. No need to be afraid...Come to Me...If you but knew how dearly I love you.

And you, dear souls, why this coldness and indifference on your part?...Do I not know that family cares...household concerns...and the requirements of your position in life make continual calls upon you?

...But cannot you spare a few minutes in which to come and prove your affection and your gratitude? Do not allow yourselves to be involved in useless and incessant cares, but spare a few moments to visit and receive this Prisoner of Love!

(*Could You Not Watch with Me One Hour - How to Cultivate a Deeper Relationship with the Lord through Eucharistic Adoration* quoting Sister Josefa Menendez)

However incredible may appear the love which the Son of God shows us in the Adorable Eucharist, there is something else yet more surprising. It is the ingratitude with which we repay so great a love. It is marvelous, indeed, that Jesus Christ should take delight in loving man. But it is most unaccountable that man should not love Jesus Christ, and that no motive, no benefit, no excess of love can inspire Him with the least feeling of gratitude. Jesus Christ may perhaps have some reason for loving men. They are His work. In them He loves His own gifts. In loving them He loves Himself.

(*Devotion to the Sacred Heart* – Father John Croiset, S.J.)

When you come into My presence to adore Me, and prefer Me to the other things that solicit your attention and make claims upon your time, I am consoled and glorified.

The proof of friendship is the choice of one's friend over all else. I want you to prefer Me, to give Me time that could be given to other persons and things. In so doing, you will show Me your love and offer Me the consolation of a true friendship.

I would ask this preferential love of all My priests. Friendship, if it is to thrive, must be practiced. This is as true of friendship with Me as it is of human friendships. I wait for the companionship of My priests.

(In Sinu Iesu - When Heart Speaks to Heart - The Journal of a Priest)

I find my consolation in the only companion of mine who never leaves me, that is, our Divine Savior in the Holy Eucharist.

It is at the foot of the altar that we find the strength we need in our isolation. Without the Blessed Sacrament, a situation like mine would not be sustainable. But with our Lord at my side, well then! I continue to be always happy and content. With this gaiety of heart and a smile on my lips, I work with zeal for the good of the poor unfortunate lepers, and little by little, without much fuss, good is done …[Jesus in the Blessed Sacrament] is the most tender of friends with souls that seek to please Him. His goodness knows how to proportion itself to the littlest of His creatures as to the greatest. Do not fear, then, in solitary conversations, to speak to Him of your woes, your fears, your troubles, those who are dear to you, your plans, your hopes; do it confidently and with an open heart.'

(*Could You Not Watch with Me One Hour - How to Cultivate a Deeper Relationship with the Lord through Eucharistic Adoration* quoting Saint Damien of Molokai)

Let us never forget that an age prospers or dwindles in proportion to its devotion to the Holy Eucharist. This is the measure of its spiritual life and its faith, of its charity and its virtue.

(Saint Peter Julian Eymard)

Be a Eucharistic soul! If the center around which your thoughts and hopes turn is the Tabernacle, then, my child, how abundant the fruits of your sanctity and apostolate will be!

(Saint Josemaria Escriva)

It is happiness to be in heaven, no doubt, because it is to be with Jesus; but have we not almost the same happiness here? Do we not possess Him in the Most Holy Sacrament? Did we but know how to profit by His Divine Presence, we should in some way have no reason to envy the inhabitants of the Heavenly City.

(Marie Estelle Harpain)

Our Redeemer ever present in the most Blessed Sacrament, extends His hands to everyone. He opens His heart and says, 'Come to Me, all of you.'

(Saint Raphael Kalinowski, O.C.D.)

Consider, on your knees, the mystery of God's love for us, that He didn't want to leave us orphans...For Christ knew our hunger for Himself. He knew that we would be walking around in the darkness of a thousand wars and miseries throughout this life...This is Holy Thursday. This is when the Christ we are talking about took an ordinary piece of bread and little wine and changed it into his Body and his Blood... Remember this day always, year after year: the day of Christ's infinite love, when He went away and yet He remained, in Bread and Wine.

(Catherine Doherty, Servant of God)

Receiving Communion is not like picturing with the imagination, as when we reflect upon the Lord on the cross or in other episodes of the passion. In Communion, the event is happening now, and it is entirely true.

(Saint Teresa of Avila)

Kneeling in this way [adoration] is the bodily expression of our positive response to the Real Presence of Jesus Christ, who as God and man, with body and soul, flesh and blood is present among us.

(Pope Emeritus Benedict XVI)

If you receive Him [Jesus in the Holy Eucharist], you are like the Virgin Mary during the months she carried her child. You truly carry Christ within you and want to be absorbed in profound thanksgiving. You carry Him living within you! How necessary is silence so that the Holy Spirit can reveal to us the grandeur of this mystery.

(Servant of God, Pere Jacques de Jesus Bunel)

If you want to experience true peace, come to the Tabernacle. Oh, what love you will feel. My Father waits for you. He waits until you are ready to sit and honor His Son. He waits for you to open your heart: to believe He is there, so that He can give you the warmth of His Love and His Peace. For if you believe I am there, all things are possible. What happened? Your families before you, honored Me. They sat with Me, talked with Me. Churches were full, and because of their love for Me, and the one who sent Me, they did all they could for my Church. A lot has happened in the last 30 years. I am the same God, yet there is no reverence for Me or my Son. You come with your hands in your pockets, not folded in prayer; children eat, laugh and play in the Real Presence of My Son. Some look away, as if they don't know what to do; most don't know who I am. Come to the Tabernacle and learn who I am. I am Love, Peace and Joy in your times of darkness, in your times of sorrow. I have always loved you. Do you remember, I died for you?

Come, come to the Tabernacle so that I can teach you Who I am.

(Saint Teresa of the Andes)

All you have loved in me comes from the time I spent in front of the Blessed Sacrament. All that has disappointed you in me comes from the time I should have spent in front of the Blessed Sacrament.

(*Could You Not Watch with Me One Hour? - How to Cultivate a Deeper Relationship with the Lord through Eucharistic Adoration* - Father Florian Racine)

...You, Jesus Christ become Man; You bread! Oh, to annihilate oneself, how little that would be! If you had left us a relic of Yourself it would be a sign of love worthy of our veneration, but you yourself remain knowing that you would be the object of profanation, sacrilege and ingratitude, abandoned. Are you, Lord, made with love?

It is horrible irreverence to Him who with so much love and sweetness invites us to perfection, to say, 'I do not want to be holy, or perfect, or to have a greater share in Your friendship, or to follow the counsels You give me to advance in it'.

(Saint Francis de Sales)

How your life would change if you went to Him often as a friend. Can you be thinking Jesus won't want to welcome you as a friend? If that's what you thought, it would be a sign you don't know Him. Jesus is all tenderness, all love for His sinful creatures. He lives in the tabernacle with His Heart open to receive us, waiting for our arrival so He may console us.

(Saint Teresa of the Andes)

Jesus Christ, during his life on earth, never passed by anywhere without pouring out His abundant blessings, from which we can deduce how great and precious must be the gifts which those who have the happiness of receiving Him in Holy Communion must share, or rather, that all the happiness we can have in this life consists in receiving Our Lord in Holy Communion.

(Saint John Vianney)

What shall we do, you sometimes ask, in the presence of Jesus in the Blessed Sacrament? Love Him, praise Him, thank Him and ask Him for things. What does a thirsty person do when he sees a pure clean fountain?

(Saint Alphonsus Liguori)

[The Seraphim] know that the greatest sin of society is not the sin of the flesh, not the sin of man against man, or of man against woman, or even of man and woman against mankind. These sins cry to Heaven for vengeance, it is true; but the sin that is at the root of all these, the sin of all sins is the neglect of God by man.

(A Trappist author)

If we were naturally good and naturally progressive, there would have been no need of Christ coming to earth to make men good. Those who are well have no need of a physician. If all were right with the world, God would have stayed in His Heaven. His Presence in the crib in Bethlehem is a witness not to our progress, but to our misery. Just as Christmas is a season for exchanging gifts with friends, so Our Lord came to this poor earth of ours to exchange gifts. He said to us, as only a good God could say: 'You give Me your humanity and I will give you My divinity; you give Me your time and I will give you My eternity; you give Me your weary body and I will give you redemption; you give Me your broken heart and I will give you love; you give Me your nothingness and I will give you My All'.

(Venerable Fulton J. Sheen)

What would happen, O my Lord God, Jesus Christ, if You made the light of Your Divinity to shine from Your most Holy Sacrament, when the priest brings It in his hands to a sick person? Before this light, all would encounter It or see It would fall prostrate on the ground spontaneously, just as the angels cover their faces before this Sacrament. While on the other hand, so many treat this heavenly Sacrament with indifference.

(*Dominus Est – It is the Lord!* - Most Reverend Athanasius Schneider, quoting Saint John Kronstadt)

Every night, after his friars had gone to bed, Saint Dominic would go to the church, and there, near the Lord, spend the long exacting hours of the night in prayer where he found interior consolation, solace, secret joys, ineffable delights, which our Lord poured out from His enchanting Heart in this holy Sacrament of love

(*Hidden Treasure* - Louis Kaczmarek)

It must not be so much the grandeur and majesty of God which causes wonder before the Eucharistic mystery, but rather His condescension and love.

(Father Raniero Cantalamessa)

O marvelous Sacrament! How can I find the words to praise You! You are the life of the soul, the medicine healing our wounds, our Comforter when we are overburdened, the

the memorial of Jesus Christ, the proof of His love, the most precious precept of His testament, our companion in the pilgrimage of life, the joy sustaining us in our exile, the burning coal kindling the fire of Divine love, the instrument of grace, the pledge of eternal bliss and the treasure of Christians.

(Venerable Louis of Granada, O.P.)

When I see people going down on both knees before the Blessed Sacrament exposed, I experience such happiness in my love for our Lord that I sometimes shed tears. It seems to me that I adore our Savior in the persons of all those who kneel before Him. I accompany in my inmost soul those external acts which honor His Divine majesty. I say in my own mind: 'Yes, the Lamb that was slain is worthy to receive all glory and honor. O my soul, prostrate yourself still more!' I adore Him with each worshipper after another. May He be known, praised, and exalted by those whom He has purchased with His Precious Blood!

(Saint Eugene de Mazenod)

It is nightfall...One by one the lights go out in the dwellings of men...Millions of stars twinkle in the vast vault of heaven...But on earth one only star still glimmers - the tiny star of light in the sanctuary lamp. Its feeble rays struggle through the windows of a little church...it moves unsteadily to and fro...until it reaches you...Do you not see it? Jesus sends it to tell you that He never rests, that day and night, year in and year out, His heart is busy loving you, and the poor, and the unhappy - yes, even those who crucify Him.

(*Eucharistic Whisperings* - Father Winfrid Herbst, S.D.S.)

Simeon gave back Jesus to His Mother, he was only suffered to keep Him for one moment. But we are far happier than Simeon. We may keep Him always if we will. In Communion, He comes not only into our arms but into our hearts.

(Saint John Vianney)

Give me the grace to long for Your Holy Sacraments, and especially to rejoice in the presence of Your body, sweet Savior Christ, in the Holy Sacrament of the altar.

(Saint Thomas More)

The same Savior, whom the written word presents to our eyes on all the paths He trod on earth in human form, lives among us disguised in the form of the Eucharistic bread.

(Saint Teresa Benedicta of the Cross)

Let Jesus present in the Blessed Sacrament speak to your hearts. It is He Who is the true answer of life that you seek! Seek Him without tiring, welcome Him without reserve, love Him without interruption; today, tomorrow, forever!

(Saint John Paul II)

To every soul that visits Jesus in the Most Holy Sacrament, He addresses the words which He said to the Sacred Spouse: 'Arise, make haste, my love, my dove, my beautiful one, and

Come' (Cant. ii. 10). You, O soul, that visits me, 'arise' from your miseries; I am here to enrich you with graces. 'Make haste,' approach, come near Me; fear not My majesty which has humbled Itself in this Sacrament in order to take away your fear, and to give you confidence. 'My beloved,' you are no longer My enemy, but My friend since you love Me and I love you...

Lord Jesus, You are in the Holy Eucharist. You are there a yard away in the tabernacle. Your body, Your soul, Your human nature, Your Divinity, Your whole being is there in its twofold nature. How close you are my God, my Savior, my Jesus, my Brother, my Spouse, my Beloved.

(Caryll Houselander)

Oh, Jesus present in the Blessed Sacrament in our churches, You give us solace and refuge; You give us faith, hope, love and hospitality. You build for us an inner retreat, an ardent repose. Help us to seek You and find You in the tabernacle.

(Blessed Charles de Foucauld)

Be convinced that there is in all your life no more precious time than that of Holy Communion and the moments following, during which you have the happiness to be able to speak face to face, heart to heart, with Jesus.

(Saint John Baptist de la Salle)

With all the strength of my soul I urge you young people to approach the Communion table as often as you can. Feed on this bread of angels whence you will draw all the energy you need to fight inner battles. Because true happiness, dear friends, does not consist in pleasures of the world or in earthly things, but in peace of conscience, which we have only if we are pure in heart and mind.

(Blessed Pier Giorgio Frassati)

Mary, adoring her God present in the Eucharist, shed abundant tears. At sight of those who make no account of this august sacrifice of the altar and so render fruitless this mystery of their redemption; at sight of those who dare to sin against, to despise this adorable Victim offered under their very eyes for their salvation. Mary, as the best of all mothers, instead of rejecting and execrating these sinners, took upon herself the penalty of their crimes. She expiated them by suffering; she became a victim at the foot of the altar, imploring grace and mercy for her guilty children.

(Saint Peter Julian Eymard)

What would your wife say if you were a whole month without showing her any marks of affection? She would say that you do not love her. You would cause trouble in your home. Well, when you do not receive Communion, God says to Himself that you do not love Him. And there is trouble in your soul.

(Saint Andre Bessette)

The best model for our thanksgiving [after Holy Communion] is Mary receiving the Word in her womb. The most pleasing reception we can make Jesus and the one best and most rich in graces for us is to join with His Blessed Mother in adoring Him present in our hearts.

(Saint Peter Julian Eymard)

Arouse Venerable Brethren, in the hearts of those committed to your care, a great and insatiable hunger for Jesus Christ. Under your guidance, let the children and youth crowd to the altar rails to offer themselves, their innocence and their works of zeal to the Divine Redeemer.

(*Mediator Dei* - Venerable Pope Pius XII)

When you see It [the Body of Christ] exposed, say to yourself: Thanks to this body, I am no longer dust and ashes, I am no more a captive but a freeman: hence I hope to obtain heaven and the good things that are there in store for me, eternal life, the heritage of the angels, companionship with Christ; death has not destroyed this body which was pierced by nails and scourged…this is that body which was once covered with blood, pierced by a lance, from which issued saving fountains upon the world, one of blood and the other of water…This body He gave to us to keep and eat, as a mark of His intense love.

(Saint John Chrysostom)

Just as He stood quietly among His apostles, so does He abide with us in the Blessed Sacrament, that we may get to know Him, to outlive our tremulous agitation, and the novelty of our surprise, and to grow familiar with Him, if we can, as our life-long Guest. There we can bring our sorrows and cares and necessities at all hours. We can choose our own time, and our visit can be as short or as long as duties permit or as love desires. There is an unction and a power in the mere silent companionship of the Blessed Sacrament which is beyond all words.

(Father Frederick William Faber)

In making the visit [to the Blessed Sacrament], consider yourselves as representatives of humanity before the tabernacle, gathering the hearts of all men and women and children everywhere…presenting all their needs to God, asking Him to give them strength in weakness, and light in obscurity. Do this so that they may be kept far from sin, so that Jesus may conquer the resistance of sinners, so that those who are consecrated to God may be granted holiness and zeal. Jesus has given us this ministry: to represent humanity before the tabernacle. This is your vocation: a ministry of love!

(Blessed James Alberione)

We cannot separate our lives from the Eucharist; the moment we do, something breaks. People ask, 'Where do the sisters get the joy and energy to do what they are doing?' The Eucharist involves more than just receiving; it also involves satisfying the hunger of Christ. He says, 'Come to Me.' He is hungry for souls.' When the sisters are exhausted, up to their eyes in work, and all seems to go awry, they spend an hour in prayer before the Blessed Sacrament. This practice has never failed to bear fruit; they experience peace and strength.

(Saint Teresa of Calcutta)

In the course of the day, when you can do nothing else, call Jesus, even in the middle of your tasks...Fly with your spirit to the tabernacle, when you cannot do so with your body, and pour out your ardent yearnings, speak and pray and embrace the Delight of souls, and even better if you can receive it Sacramentally.

(Saint Pio of Pietrelcina)

What joy ought not we men to conceive, what hopes and what affections, in knowing that in the midst of our land, in our churches, near our houses, the Holy of Holies, the true God, dwells and lives in the Most Holy Sacrament of the Altar! He who by His presence alone renders the saints in heaven blessed! He who is love itself.

(Saint Alphonsus Liguori)

If the great event of the Second Vatican Council was a breath of the Spirit that was blown into the world through the windows of the Church, then we need to recognize that a lot of worldliness has also blown in with the Spirit, creating a current and blowing the leaves all over. We've seen everything and yet nothing has been lost, but order must be patiently restored.

Order is restored above all by strongly affirming the primacy of the Risen Christ present in the Eucharist.

There is a great peaceful battle to be waged which is that of Perpetual Eucharistic Adoration, so that the entire world can become part of a network of prayer, united to the Holy Rosary, in which we reflect on the salvific mysteries of Christ with Mary. This will generate and develop a movement of reparation and penetration.

(Cardinal Mauro Piacenza, former Prefect of the Congregation for the Clergy)

Eucharistic piety should be centered above all on the celebration of the Lord's Supper, which perpetuates the pouring out of His love on the Cross. But it has a logical prolongation…in the adoration of Christ in this Divine Sacrament, in the Visit to the Blessed Sacrament, in prayer beside the Tabernacle, as well as in those other exercises of devotion both personal and collective, private and public, which you have been practicing for centuries…Jesus waits for us in this Sacrament of Love. Let us not be mean with our time when it comes to going to meet Him in adoration, in contemplation that is filled with faith, and disposed to make reparation for the grave faults and crimes of the world.

(Saint John Paul II - Address, October 31, 1982)

It [Eucharistic Adoration] is a time of encounter between the depths of our misery and the depths of God's love. It is there that I can know that I am loved by Christ who delivered Himself for me. Everything is from Him. He knows how to untie the knots that keep me in their grip. There, I to be silent in the deepest part of myself in order to be transformed by the Holy Spirit, real problems resolving themselves at the foot of the tabernacle. Jesus said to Angela of Foligno: 'Concern yourself with me, and I will concern myself with you.' Adoration nourishes faith, trains it to avoid lapsing into unbelief or superstition. It is essential among this people that believes that it is being injured. Adoration is not a pharmacy but the gratuitousness of God's gift.

(*Could You Not Watch With Me One Hour – How To Cultivate a Deeper Relationship With the Lord Through Eucharistic Adoration,* quoting Archbishop Kébreau of Cap-Haltien)

A saint said that we were Christ-bearers. It is very true; but we have not enough faith. We do not comprehend our dignity. When we leave the holy banquet, we are as happy as the Wise Men would have been, if they could have carried away the Infant Jesus. Take a vessel full of liquor, and cork it well - you will keep the liquor as long as you please. So, if you were to keep Our Lord well and recollectedly after Communion, you would long feel that devouring fire which would inspire your heart with an inclination to good and a repugnance to evil.

(Saint John Vianney)

Let us imagine that the Communion, for which we are preparing, is to be the last in our lives. Let us prepare, every time, as though, on quitting the holy table, we had to pass from this life to eternity. If we desire that the Sacrament of the Eucharist should produce in us sentiments of the love of God, let us think of the immense love which God has shown us in instituting this mystery, and of His design to oblige us thereby to love Him perfectly.

The reproof of Jesus Christ to Martha for too great solicitude, should teach some souls, who are disquieted and wholly taken up with reciting many vocal prayers, that tranquility of heart, interior recollection and attention in listening, from time to time, to Jesus Christ in silence, like Magdalen, is the best preparation we can make.

So that we should employ the greater part of the precious time that precedes, accompanies and immediately follows Communion, in making many interior acts, of which the love of Jesus Christ should be the principle, and the increase of this love the chief effect.

(*Devotion to the Sacred Heart* - Father John Croiset, S.J.)

If Holy Communion is the most intimate union of the soul with God, how fervent would [the Blessed Mother's] Communions be! It would seem to her that the Incarnation was renewed in every Holy Communion. On receiving Jesus, she would again feel the effective, real and true Presence of her Son. Not a day would pass without her receiving Our Lord. Her Holy Communion would be the central action of every day. The whole day would seem far too short for her preparation and thanksgiving. If the saints say that only one Holy Communion would suffice to make a saint, what effects would it have on the soul of Our Lady? In certain souls, the effects of their devout Holy Communions are conspicuous. Let us try, then, to imagine what Holy Communion meant for the Immaculate Mother of God. We should also center our lives around the Holy Eucharist. Holy Communion, Holy Hours, and Visits to the Blessed Sacrament must be the most important acts of our lives. Let us remember Mary, let us imitate her, pray to her, entreat her not to abandon us; and let us ask her to teach us how to receive Holy Communion well.

(*The Last Years of Our Lady* - Saint John Eudes)

The night before [Jesus] died He said 'This is my body – This is my blood'. Every day that we live, we are to hold out on the paten of our hands, our hearts, and minds, and wills, our all, and say: 'This is my body - this is my blood.' Take them. And what You do with wheat and wine and these awe-filled words, do with me! Let the outward appearances remain; my face, figure, height, and breadth; but the inner substance, change! Change it so that it will no longer be mine, but Thine. Change it so that I will always be what transubstantiated Wheat and Wine ever remain – Thee.

(*God, A Woman and The Way* - Rev. M. Raymond, O.C.S.O.)

Get to know our Lord better. Study His life, His sacrifices, and His virtues in the Most Blessed Sacrament. Study His love. Instead of always remaining within ourselves, let us go up to Him; it is all very well to see ourselves in Him, but to see Him in us is better. Instead of attending to yourself, attend to our Lord and make Him grow in you. Think of Him; study Him in Himself; penetrate into Him. You will find the food of your life in Him; for He is great and infinite. That is the broad and royal road to holiness and the way to the ennobling of our lives.

(Saint Peter Julian Eymard)

If you had a burning lamp and all the world came to you for light, the light of your lamp would not be diminished by the sharing, yet each person who shared it would have the whole light. True, each one's light would be more or less intense depending on what sort of material each brought to receive the fire. I give you this example so that you may better understand me. Imagine that many people brought candles, and one person's candle weighed one ounce, another's more.

Still, you would think that the person who carried the one-ounce candle would have less than the one whose candle weighed a pound. Well, this is how it goes with those who receive this Sacrament. Each one of you brings your own candle, that is, the holy desire with which you receive and eat this Sacrament. Your candle by itself is unlit, and it is lighted when you receive this Sacrament. I say it is unlit because by yourselves you are nothing at all. It is I who have given you the candle with which you can receive this light and nourish it within you. And your candle is love, because it is for love that I created you, so without love you cannot have life.

It is with this love that you come to receive my gracious light, the light I have given you as food, to be administered to you by my ministers. But even though all of you receive the light, each of you receives it in proportion to the love and burning desire you bring with you. Each of you carries the light whole and undivided, for it cannot be divided by any imperfection in you who receive it or in those who administer it. You share as much of the light (that is, the grace you receive in this Sacrament) as your holy desire disposes you to receive.

(*The Dialogue* - God the Father to Saint Catherine of Siena)

So immense are its spiritual benefits that Pope Saint Pius X hailed perpetual adoration as the devotion which surpasses all others. And Paul VI had it mainly in mind when he echoed the hope generated by Vatican II that a 'new era of Eucharistic piety would pervade the whole Church.' As we would expect, an outstanding spiritual growth and impetus tend to spring from perpetual adoration. It brings heaven's choice blessings in the first place on those generous souls that keep their hour-long tryst with the Lord. But, being such a powerhouse of grace, the devotion extends its influence far beyond the individual adorers, touching their homes and families and reaching out to the parish community and beyond.

(Father Richard Foley, S. J.)

When Christ manifested Himself to Margaret Mary, and declared to her the infinitude of His love, at the same time, in the manner of a mourner, He complained that so many and such great injuries were done to Him by ungrateful men — and we would that these words in which He made this complaint were fixed in the minds of the faithful, and were never blotted out by oblivion:

'Behold this Heart' — He said — 'which has loved men so much and has loaded them with all benefits, and for this boundless love has had no return but neglect, and contumely, and this often from those who were bound by a debt and duty of more special love.'

In order that these faults might be washed away, He then recommended several things to be done, and in particular the following as most pleasing to Himself, namely that men should approach the Altar with this purpose of expiating sin, making what is called a Communion of Reparation — and that they should likewise make expiatory supplications and prayers, prolonged for a whole hour — which is rightly called the 'Holy Hour.'

(*Miserentissimus Redemptor* - Pope Pius XI)

In order to be like You, who are always alone in the Blessed Sacrament, I shall love solitude and try to converse with You as much as possible. Grant that my mind may not seek to know anything but You, that my heart may have no longings or desires but to love You. When I am obliged to take some comfort, I shall take care to see that it be pleasing to Your Heart.

In my conversations, O divine Word, I shall consecrate all my words to You so that You will not permit me to pronounce a single one which is not for Your glory...When I am thirsty, I shall endure it in honor of the thirst You endured for the salvation of souls...If by chance, I commit some fault, I shall humble myself, and then take the opposite virtue from Your Heart, offering it to the eternal Father in expiation for my failure.

All this I intend to do, O Eucharistic Jesus, to unite myself to You in every action of the day.

(Saint Margaret Mary Alacoque – Missionaries of the Blessed Sacrament)

After this [Jesus telling His followers that he who feeds on His flesh and drinks His blood has eternal life] many of His disciples went back and walked no more with Him. Then Jesus said to the twelve: Will you also go away?

This question came from a Heart so inflamed with love, and was in itself so strong a proof of excessive tenderness, that it could not fail to oblige those, to whom it was directed, to love Jesus Christ yet more ardently.

It had also all the effect that this Divine Savior desired; and this increase of fervor in the Apostles, consoled Him a little, for the affliction He felt, at the departure of those who had forsaken Him. Jesus Christ often asks us the same question, and for the same reason. How happy should we be, if it had the same effect!

Every day this loving Savior sees Himself forsaken by those unhappy creatures, who, tired of His benefits, withdraw themselves from His service. He is left alone.

Faithful servants, fervent Christians, hear the question put to you by Jesus Christ: 'And you,' He says, 'will you abandon Me? Are you disgusted with this divine, food, and tired of My service? Will you act like those who go away, and come only with the crowd, to offer Me their homage mechanically, or to pass the time?'

(*Devotion to The Sacred Heart* - Father John Croiset, S.J.)

The Eucharist must be the source and center of our lives. If we and our priests prefer Him over all others and all things, He will transform us and our world - one heart at a time. We can never share this Truth enough!

(*Vultus Christi*)

Oh, how sweet was the conversation I held with Paradise this morning. The Heart of Jesus and my own, if you will pardon my expression, fused. They were no longer two hearts beating but only one. My heart disappeared as if it were a drop in the ocean.

(Saint Pio of Pietrelcina - Missionaries of the Blessed Sacrament)

However, terrible the state of your soul may seem to you, however unfortunate or even guilty you may feel, do not shy from Him, do not lose courage but cling to your Jesus even as a drowning man clings to a rope. Stay near the Host for His Heart is ever watchful. Who can tear you away if you do not wish to leave? Has He not said, that He himself will be your Defender? Remember His Word has never deceived anyone.

I implore you, do not listen to Satan who wishes to drive you away. Stay with Jesus who is there in the Sacred Host, for from Him even as in the days of His mortal life, there will come forth that powerful virtue which heals and saves.

It is for you that He is there, for you that He offers His Blood, His Wounds, and His Merits. It is when you are there prostrate at His feet, that His Blood flows over your soul, that He covers you with His Merits, that He hides you in His Wounds and in His Heart

.

If you but understood the gift of God, if you but knew Him who waits for you all day long even as He waited at the well of Jacob for the Samaritan woman, you would realize that it is there that He has desired to cover you with His protection and His love, it is there that He wishes to be your Savior and your Friend, it is from there that He will come to you in your last hour if you have gone to Him during your life and it is there that He will receive you into His Heart to conduct you to eternal happiness.

(My Eucharistic Day: Rules and Practices Recommended by Saint Peter Eymard)

Even after three years of close companionship with Jesus, the apostles noticed no striking change in each other, and little in themselves. Yet Jesus saw a steady transformation going forward, and He rejoiced. He saw how the love of Himself, which brings with it all good, was gradually raising their standards; was widening, purifying, and kindling their hearts; and preparing the material for fire which at Pentecost was to descend upon them and transform them into other men. Slowly and quietly, as is the way with the works of God, the apostles grew into the knowledge of the likeness of the Son of God, until each in his measure of capacity, and according to God's plan for him became *alter Christus* — another Christ. So it will be with us."

(*The Blessed Sacrament Prayer Book* - Mother Mary Loyola

When a preacher or catechist retains in himself the warm life of the Precious Blood, when his heart is consumed with the fire that consumes the Eucharistic Heart of Jesus, what life his words will have: they will burn, they will be living flames! And what effects the Eucharist will have, radiating throughout a class for instance, or through a hospital ward, or in a club, and so on, when the ones God has chosen to work there have nourished their zeal in Holy Communion, and have become Christ-bearers!

(*The Soul of The Apostolate* - Jean Baptiste Chautard, O.C.S.O.)

Were we to communicate only once in our life, our whole life, however long it might be, would not be too long to prepare ourselves worthily for receiving so holy and so awful a mystery. This should not, however, keep us from it. It should only urge us to approach it with the requisite dispositions. We are wrong, then, when we say: 'I will not communicate, because I feel I am unworthy.' We should say, on the contrary: 'I will endeavor, as far as possible, by the innocence and regularity of my life, to make myself worthy to communicate.'

To approach worthily, is to believe ourselves unworthy; while, at the same time, we do what we can to make ourselves less unworthy. A single good Communion is enough to make a Saint. Not much more is necessary than a good will, and a few reflections, in order to make a good Communion.

Those who communicate often without becoming more devout, more mortified, more recollected, without loving Jesus Christ more and more, are in a more dangerous state than they think. What would have been said, if those who often conversed with Jesus Christ, and usually ate at His table, had not become daily more virtuous? What further hope would there have been for those sick persons who were presented to Jesus Christ, if Jesus Christ had not cured them?

(Devotion to The Sacred Heart- - Father John Croiset, S.J.).

Priests, yes, even My priests, are sometimes fearful of finding themselves silent and alone in My presence. When they come to adore Me and to offer Me the consolation of their company, I do not require that they speak to Me; it is enough that they remain in the radiance of My Eucharistic Face, allowing their hearts to reach out to My Eucharistic Heart.

Those who have experienced this movement of the heart to My Eucharistic Heart will know of what I speak. Words are not always necessary. The engagement of the heart, on the other hand, is indispensable.

Weariness and fatigue are no obstacle to a fruitful time of adoration. They are incidental; what matters is the desire to seek My Eucharistic Face and to abide in My company.

For one who loves, the time in My presence passes quickly, storing up immense treasures of merit for souls. The merits of your adoration I consider as belonging to the neediest and most broken of My priests.

(In Sinu Iesu – When Heart Speaks to Heart - The Journal of a Priest)

My God, You are my life; if I leave You, I cannot but thirst. Lost spirits thirst in hell, because they have not God. They thirst, though they would have it otherwise, from the necessity of their original nature. But I, my God, wish to thirst for You with a better thirst. I wish to be clad in that new nature, which so longs for You from loving You, as to overcome in me the fear of coming to You. I come to You, 0 Lord, not only because I am unhappy without You, not only because I feel I need You, but because Your grace draws me on to seek You for Your own sake, because You are so glorious and beautiful.

I come in great fear, but in greater love. O may I never lose, as years pass away, and the heart shuts up, and all things are a burden, let me never lose this youthful, eager, elastic love of You. Make Your grace supply the failure of nature. Do the more for me, the less I can do for myself. The more I refuse to open my heart to You, so much the fuller and stronger be Your supernatural visitations, and the more urgent and efficacious Your presence in me.

(You My Soul Has Thirsted - Blessed John Henry Cardinal Newman)

It seems as though Jesus Christ would have been more loved had He loved us less. I shudder with horror, oh my God, at the mere thought of the indignities and outrages which the impiety of wicked Christians, and the fury of heretics, have committed against this august Sacrament. With what horrible sacrileges have not our Altars and our Churches been profaned? With what repeated insults, impiety and infamy, has not the Body of Jesus Christ been treated? Can any Christian reflect on such impiety, without conceiving an ardent desire to repair by 'every possible means' these cruel outrages? Is it possible, then, that he should live without giving it a thought?

If, amidst the impiety which Jesus Christ meets with at the hands of heretics, He at least were honored and ardently loved by the faithful, we might in some degree console ourselves for the outrages of the one, by the love and sincere homage of the other. But alas! Where are we to look for that crowd of adorers, earnestly bent on honoring Jesus Christ in our Churches? Are not our Churches deserted? Can there be greater coldness and indifference than what is shown towards Jesus Christ in the Blessed Sacrament? The scant number that are to be seen in our Churches during the greater part of the day, are they not a visible proof of the forgetfulness and want of love of almost all Christians? Those who approach our Altars most frequently, familiarize themselves with these most august mysteries. It may be said, that there are Priests, whose familiarity to Jesus Christ goes so far as to grow into indifference and contempt.

(*Devotion to The Sacred Heart* - Father John Croiset, S.J.)

When Jesus remains in the quiet of the altar, in the tabernacle's shadow, people in their blind carelessness let

Him alone, they forget all about Him. And when He exposes Himself upon the altar, He is hurt to the Heart by the irreverence of so many who either have no faith at all or a faith that is very weak. When He goes through the streets in order to bring unspeakable blessings to His beloved children, He hears curses and blasphemies that make out of His errand of mercy another way of the cross.

But in the midst of all these bitternesses one hope sustains Him – the hope of a place of refuge that will offer the love and peace He craves. The bitter chalice which others continually place to His lips He drinks with resignation; for He is sustained by the hope of a loving reception in my heart by way of reparation. One holy hour spent in the enjoyment of my love, and He forgets years and years of suffering…

Altar and tabernacle, monstrance and church, are merely the avenues through which His love enters; its goal is my heart; it is there that He would rest. Ah! How it would pain His Divine Heart if I would not let Him in, or if I would receive Him unworthily. What a bitter disappointment that would be!

(*Eucharistic Whisperings* - Father Winfrid Herbst, S.D.S.)

My Eucharistic Jesus, I love You more now that I hide myself so that You may appear...now that I conceal myself so that You may reign...now that I am nothing so that You may be everything.

I love You more, much more, adorable Jesus...now that I have died to earth's vanities...now that, with Your grace, I have moved away from worldly things...now that I have renounced being something that was not trash...now that I have stood in the shade so that others could shine!

I love You more now that I keep my soul clean…now that I am voluntarily poor…now that I obey and crucify myself to please You.

Is it not true, my Jesus, that all of this is the fruit of solitude, and that at the foot of Your Sacrament one enjoys an intimacy that is unknown to the world because of its purity? Here, let me stay very near to You, Jesus of my life! Caresses and tenderness flow night and day in the midst of pain and tears…Here my sighs burn You and Your glances scorch me…Here I hand You my pain and You envelope me in Your love.

O Jesus, Eucharistic Jesus! In this silence and solitude that surrounds us, my heart bursts forth with all the fire of the love that You communicate to me, and which consumes me…

O Eucharistic Jesus! Here I tell you my sorrows, my sins, my bitterness, the misery of my soul, and my feeble response.

Here, I also hear Your complaints, Your rebukes, Your desires, Your teachings and Your forgiveness. Mutually, we dry our tears from our souls, and the world ignores what only the angels contemplate.

I offer You my joys, I let You share in my sorrows, and You sweeten everything with Your touch.

(Holy Hours - Concepcion Cabrera de Armida)

What is a church, be it large or small, without a sanctuary lamp? Is it not like a body without a soul? When entering a church, a Catholic instinctively lets his eyes roam over the sanctuary in search of that tiny flame of light; and if he finds it not, he seems to hear in the depths of his heart a little voice that is cold and disappointing: 'Your Savior is not here!' It may be that rare treasures of art are gathered together there; but of what avail are the greatest masterpieces of the painter's brush or the sculptor's chisel if the beams of this dear light do not fall upon them? The art of man may indeed cross the threshold of our sacred edifices; it may exert all its skill for the glorification of God and the beautifying of our churches; but if this trembling light does not cast its magic rays upon them, not even the greatest genius can infuse into the marble its proper expression or give true life to the canvas.

Little sanctuary lamp, you are for me as the eye of Divine love, which penetrates to the very depths of my soul, searches out its every secret, conquers my heart, and awakens its tenderest emotions! You are always, silent, and yet – how eloquent you are!

(From *Eucharistic Whisperings* - Father Winfrid Herbst, S.D.S.)

If we really loved the good God, we should make it our joy and happiness to come and spend a few moments to adore Him, and ask Him for the grace of forgiveness; and we should regard those moments as the happiest of our lives.

(Saint John Vianney)

The efficacy of an apostolate almost invariably corresponds to the degree of Eucharistic life acquired by a soul. Indeed, the sure sign of a successful apostolate is when it makes souls thirst for frequent and fruitful participation in the Divine Banquet. And this result will never be obtained except in proportion as the apostle himself really makes Jesus in the Blessed Sacrament the source and center of his life.

Like Saint Thomas Aquinas, who practically entered the Tabernacle, so to speak, when he wanted to work out a problem, the apostle also will go and tell all his troubles to the Divine Guest, and his action upon souls will be simply his conversations with the Author of Life put into practice.

(The Soul of the Apostolate - Jean-Baptiste Chautard, O.C.S.O.)

Without the Holy Eucharist, earth would seem to us empty, the temple of God desolate, the soul cold, the heart isolated. Oh God, this earth is a vale of tears where I weep and sigh! Here I cannot remain alone – alone with people who are careless and indifferent to my suffering; I have need of Thee.

(The Holy Eucharist: Our All - Father Lukas Etlin, O.S.B.)

It is extraordinary that there are to be found Christians, and those not a few, who grow weary and do not know what to do at Mass.

Can a sick man be tired of seeing the efforts made to cure him? Or can a person, loaded with debts, find it difficult to know what to do, in the presence of a powerful monarch who has offered him all his treasures?

You do not know what to do at Mass? How is this? says Father la Colombiere, in his Reflections on this subject; have you never received any favor from God? Alas, we are surrounded, loaded, overwhelmed with His benefits, and we have never thanked Him as we ought.

At Mass, at least, give a thought to these various benefits; so many sins over-looked, so loving a Providence continually exercised in your regard, so sweet and so constant an effort to draw you to Him, to gain your heart, to make you holy. The graces that you receive in one single day would suffice to occupy you during the whole of Mass. Is not all this deserving of your remembrance?

But what can I render Thee, oh Lord, for having given me the means of acknowledging so liberally the benefits of Thy Father, the means of expiating all my sins? I have only one heart to offer Thee. Wilt Thou deign to accept this heart, agitated by so many passions, and defiled with so many sins? It is at least broken with grief, and in this state, I offer it to Thee. Thou opens to me Thine own; shall I dare, my loving Savior, to refuse Thee mine? O God of majesty! who am I, that Thou should deign to accept this sacrifice of my heart? It shall then be all Thine.

(*Devotion to the Sacred Heart* - Father John Croiset, S.J.)

And yet we have talked to them about the joys of religion and of good conscience. But because we have not known how to slake our own thirst at the living waters of the Lamb, we have mumbled and stuttered in our attempts to portray those ineffable joys, the very desire of which would have shattered the chains of the triple concupiscence much more effectively than all our thundering tirades about hell...Our lips have been unable to speak the language of the Heart of Him Who loves men, because our converse with Him has been as infrequent as it has been cold.

Let us not try to shift all the blame onto the profoundly demoralized state of society. After all, we have only to look, for example, at the effect on completely de-Christianized parishes of the presence of sensible, active, devoted, capable priests, but priests who were, above all, lovers of the Eucharist.

(*The Soul of The Apostolate* - Jean Baptiste Chautard, O.C.S.O.)

Ever since the day you were born, My child, I am at your door desiring your whole heart, but…has it been Mine? …How many times have you harshly closed the door in My Face, preferring the world…the vanities…the occupations…worldly creatures…even Satan disguised?

Look back and tell Me, if you can, that it has not been so.

How could I, a poor sinner, who have so often offended You, dare to approach You, O Lord, if I beheld You in all your majesty? Under the appearance of bread, however, it is easy to approach You, for if a king disguises himself, it seems as if we do not have to talk to him with so much circumspection and ceremony. If you were not hidden, O Lord, who would dare to approach You with such coldness, so unworthily, and with so many imperfections?

(*The Way of Perfection* - Saint Teresa of Avila)

Since you came to console Me, do not end this Holy Hour without recalling here at My feet those favorites of My merciful Heart, the fallen, the prodigals, those who have wandered from the fold. Numberless they pass before this Host which veils Me from your eyes.

How they march, the haughty who insult My annihilation, the blasphemers who cover Me with opprobrium, the apostates and the impious, who come up to Me with the gall of sarcasm on their lips. How great the legion of ingrates, of those who make Me suffer by their icy indifference. Who can count them? I see them from My Tabernacle, among them, too, are My one-time friends, traitors and disloyal ones. And there are also children! Listen to Me, mothers. Yes, there are children who betray the Heart of Jesus, their great friend.

My soul is sorrowful unto death at the loss of so many poor sinners. At this very hour, many are in their agony. Therefore you, My apostles, by a fervent prayer shut the door of Hell, and open the Heaven of My Heart which awaits them with Its pardon and Its infinite mercies. Save them! They are souls that belong to Me. I entrust their salvation to you!

(*20 Holy Hours* - Rev. Mateo Crawley-Boevey, SS.CC.)

Your reasons for warning me to stay away from Holy Communion are exactly the ones which cause me to go so often. My distractions are great, but it is in Communion that I recollect myself. I have temptations many times a day. By daily Communion. I get the strength to overcome them. I have much very important business to handle and I need light and wisdom. It is for these reasons that I go to Holy Communion every day to consult Jesus about them.

(Saint Thomas More)

Adoring the Sacred Host: this ought to be the heart of every human being's life.

(Blessed Charles de Foucald)

Contemplate Me in the prison where I spent the greater part of the night. The soldiers came and, adding words to injuries, insulted Me, mocked Me, outraged Me, and gave Me blows on My face and on My whole body.

Tired of their sport, at length they left Me bound and alone in the dark and noisome place, where, seated on a stone, My aching body was cramped with cold.

Compare the prison with the Tabernacle, and especially with the hearts that receive Me. In the prison, I spent only part of the night...but in the Tabernacle, how many days and nights?

In the prison, I was insulted and ill-treated by soldiers who were my enemies. In the tabernacle, most often it is they who call Me their Father who treat Me thus, but how unlike that of children is the treatment!

In the prison I endured cold, sleeplessness, hunger and thirst, solitude, and desertion. And there passed before My mind's eye all the tabernacles where in the course of ages I should lack the shelter of love. . . the icy-cold hearts that would be as hard and unfeeling as the stones of the prison floor were to My numbed and wounded body.

And how often should I wait for this or that other soul to visit Me in the Blessed Sacrament and receive Me into his heart...how many nights should I spend longing for his coming...but he would let business or carelessness or anxiety for his health get the better of him. . . and he would not come!

O! if they would thus unite themselves to Me, with what peace would they face difficulties...how much fortitude they would win and how they would gladden My Heart!

(*The Way of Divine Love* - Our Lord to Sr. Josefa Menendez)

Eucharistic adorers share Mary's life and mission of prayer at the foot of the Most Blessed Sacrament. It is the most beautiful of all missions, and it holds no perils. It is the most holy, for in it all the virtues are practiced. It is, moreover, the most necessary to the Church, which has even more need of prayerful souls than of powerful preachers; of men of penance rather than men of eloquence. Today more than ever have we need of men who, by their self-immolation, disarm the anger of God inflamed by the ever-increasing crimes of nations. We must have souls who by their importunity re-open the treasures of grace which the indifference of the multitude has closed. We must have true adorers; that is to say, men of fervor and of sacrifice. When there are many such souls around their Divine Chief, God will be glorified, Jesus will be loved, and society will once more become Christian, conquered for Jesus Christ by the apostolate of Eucharistic prayer.

(*With Mary Let Us Adore Him!* - Saint Peter Julian Eymard)

In our visits to the Divine Solitary, we can with intense devotion prepare ourselves to receive Him sacramentally. Poor, wretched, miserable, blind, and naked, we cannot alone make ourselves fit for the reception of our God. He must clothe our souls with the wedding garment of Divine grace, and adorn them with virtue. As we kneel before the Eucharistic Savior, the Eternal Father will draw us closer to His Divine Son. Christ will so influence us as to bring out the best that is.

If Jesus Christ allows Himself to be given even to those who do not love Him, and would have Himself carried to dying persons who never condescended to visit Him in their lifetime, and who have been insensible both to the manifest marks of love which He gave them and to the cruel outrages He received in the adorable Eucharist, to persons who have perhaps themselves ill-treated Him, what will He not do for faithful servants who, sensibly touched at seeing their dear Lord so little loved, so rarely visited, so cruelly outraged, make Him atonement, from time to time, for all the insults He receives, and neglect nothing to repair so many offenses, by their frequent visits, their adorations, their homages, and chiefly their ardent love?

(*Devotion to The Sacred Heart* - Father John Croiset, S.J.)

As we kneel before the Eucharistic Savior, the Eternal Father will draw us closer to His Divine Son. Christ will so influence us as to bring out the best in us. The Holy Spirit will calm us with the peace of God, and thus remove the obstacles to our loving advance in intimate conversation with the Sacramental King. Our very nearness to Christ will dispel our diffidence at the thought of too hasty an approach to the God who has found sin among the angels. Breathing the spiritual air of the tabernacle, illumining our souls with the light reflected from His earthly dwelling, strengthening our wills for conflict with temptation, deepening our faith in His almighty power, and purifying our desire to love Him more unselfishly - how can we better prepare ourselves to receive our God with a fervor that will ever inflame us with eager enthusiasm in His service?

(*Transforming Your Life through the Eucharist* - Father John A. Kane)

CHRIST...Here upon the altar you will find not a relic, nor a monument to someone's memory, but Me, alive as ever, all-powerful, all-loving, all-perfect…All the treasures and wonders of this world – these things are nothing compared to what you find upon the altar. You will not be drawn to Me by any curiosity or shallow virtue. Only a firm faith, a steady hope, and a burning love will draw you to Me and keep you loyal to Me.

Consider how great must be the tepidity and negligence of this world, since so many fail to take advantage of My gift of Holy Communion. It is sad to see how few are drawn to Me with tender affection and wordless gratitude. In this Sacrament, I offer Myself in Whom lie all human hopes and merits for salvation.

(The Sacrifice of the Mass - Cardinal Giovanni Bona)

Beloved souls, in suffering and in joy, go to Jesus hidden in the Sacred Host and let the sweetness of His loving gaze fill you. Like the sick who expose their diseased bodies to the healing rays of the sun, expose your miseries, no matter what they are, to the beams of light streaming forth from the Sacred Host.

(Reflections and Prayers for Visits with our Eucharistic Lord - John J. Cardinal Carberry)

Let us take advantage of some guidelines given to priests on how to celebrate the Mass, in order to help us live the sacrifice with ever greater devotion:

After uttering the words which bring Christ down upon the altar, look at the Sacramental species with the eyes of faith.

As you kneel, see the legions of angels which surround Christ and adore Him with profound reverence. This sight should make you exceedingly humble.

But can we have any reason for not loving Jesus Christ, for loving Him only in a small degree, for loving anything together with Him? Is there anything, then, in Him, that keeps you from Him? Has He not yet done sufficient to merit our love? Should we ever have dared to desire, or ever have been able to imagine, all that He has deigned to do, in this adorable mystery, in order to gain our hearts? And yet all this has not been enough to oblige men to have an ardent love for Jesus Christ.

(*Devotion to The Sacred Heart* - Father John Croiset, S.J.)

I recall the strange and touching story of Saint Alexis. When he was young he left home and then, because God inspired him to do so, came back to the house of his parents in Rome dressed up like a poor and unknown beggar. There he lived in some miserable old corner of the house for seventeen years; and his parents never knew that it was he.

But when he died they found out. It seems he left a note or something telling them what he had done in penance for his sins, because God wanted him to. How that mother wept when she found out that the beggar was her son. She had missed him so much and had so longed to see him. In agony, she cried out: '0 Alexis, my son! My son Alexis! Had I only known it was you! How I would have loved you and enjoyed your company! Now, alas! it is too late.'

This is a sad story. But I am afraid that if I do not appreciate my Eucharistic Savior here on earth, where He is hidden away in the poor tabernacle, where He is in my very midst and I do not seem to know Him, the time will come, after my death, when I will cry out, seeing His adorable beauty in the life to come: '0 Jesus, if I had only known it was You! How I would have loved You, Jesus all beautiful!. How I would have enjoyed Your company! Oh, if I had only known!'

But I do know.

Faith tells me.

And I make so little of it...

(*The Way to God* - Father Winfrid Herbst S.D.S.)

Jesus Christ dwells in the midst of us in the same manner He dwelt at Nazareth amidst His relatives. He was there without being known by them, and without working in their favor, the miracles that He wrought elsewhere. Our blindness and evil dispositions prevent Him from letting us experience the wonderful operations with which He favors those whom He finds well disposed...

Why is it, then, that we have so little feeling, either for the neglect shown to Jesus Christ in the most Blessed Sacrament where He is visited by so few, or for the outrages He there endures, from the very persons who profess to believe in Him? Certainly, because the faith of Christians on this point is very weak.

It is necessary, then, to have a lively faith, in order to have this ardent love for Jesus Christ in the most Blessed Sacrament, and to be touched by a sense of the insults to which the expression of His love for us exposes Him; and to acquire, in time, a true devotion to the Sacred Heart of Jesus Christ.

In order to do this, we must lead a pure and innocent life. We must animate our faith by our assiduity, and especially by our profound respect when we present ourselves before the most Blessed Sacrament, and by every sort of good works. We must pray much, and often ask of God for this lively faith. We must, in a word, act like persons who believe, and we shall soon feel ourselves animated with this lively faith.

(*Devotion to the Sacred Heart* - Father John Croiset, S.J.)

How must we draw inspiration from Our Lord, and how obey Him in all that we do? By recalling His Presence in the Blessed Sacrament and by praying for His guidance. Do not go to seek Our Lord in heaven, for He is nearer to you than that. It is well, doubtless, to rise toward His glorious throne from time to time, and to desire to see His splendor, but in practical life, you should have Him nearer to you, and it is in the Most Blessed Sacrament that you should seek and find Him.

Our Lord might say to you: 'Why do you neglect My Presence here? Do you think it is of no importance and that you can do without it? In heaven, I am the God of glory for the elect; in My Sacrament I am the God of grace for them that struggle.'

In all your actions, then, draw your inspiration from His Eucharistic Presence. How? By adoration, by prostrating yourself in spirit at His feet, by renouncing your own natural lights, and sentiments, in order to ask of Him the how of all things. Ask of Him in everything the best means, the best thought, the best way by acknowledging your blindness and impotence.

(*The Divine Eucharist* - Saint Peter Julian Eymard

All my sermons are prepared in the presence of the Blessed Sacrament. As recreation is most pleasant and profitable in the sun, so homiletic creativity is best nourished before the Eucharist. The most brilliant ideas come from meeting God face to face. The Holy Spirit that presided at the Incarnation is the best atmosphere for illumination. Pope John Paul II keeps a small desk or writing pad near him whenever he is in the presence of the Blessed Sacrament; and I have done this all my life — I am sure for the same reason he does, because a lover always works better when the beloved is with him.

(Love Dreams - Venerable Fulton J. Sheen)

The holy Gospels tell us again and again that while the Savior was visibly with us on earth He healed the sick by His mere passing by; and with only a word, He raised the dead to life. If such were His active goodness then – and who would venture even to think of doubting it? – what works of charity must He do now, in His Eucharistic life! Oh, He does not merely pass before me now, He does not only speak to me – nay, He actually enters under my roof and transforms me into Himself.

It is not enough for Jesus to increase in me the life of grace in Holy Communion. No; He gives me even His own life. And so it appears that it is no longer I that live, but Jesus that lives within me. And therefore, it is that in the eyes of God every action of mine appears clothed in all the beauty and adorned with all the worth of the actions of Jesus.

(Eucharistic Whisperings - Father Winfrid Herbst, S.D.S.)

What happiness do we not feel in the presence of God, when we find ourselves alone at His feet before the holy Tabernacle! Come, my soul, redouble thy fervor; thou art alone adoring thy God; His eyes rest upon thee alone. This good Savior is so full of love for us, that He seeks us everywhere.

(*The Holy Eucharist Our All* - Father Lukas Etlin, O.S.B., quoting Saint John Vianney)

In the elevation, contemplate Christ elevated on the Cross. Ask Him to bring all things to Himself. Make fervent acts of faith, hope, love, adoration, humility, saying with the mind, 'Jesus, Son of God, have mercy on me! My Lord and my God I love you, my God I adore you with my whole heart and soul'. You may also renew the intention of the Mass which you are celebrating, offering up the Eucharist according to its four ends.

But when you lift up the chalice, make sure to remember in a very contrite way that the blood of Christ has been shed for you, even though you have oftentimes despised it. Adore Him so as to make up for your past neglect.

(*The Sacrifice of the Mass* - Cardinal Giovanni Bona)

Why art Thou left alone in this Most Holy Sacrament? Where are Thy adorers and Thy friends? Has Thy Church failed to announce Thy Gospel to the world, and to make Thy presence known? Why art Thou so ignored, forsaken, and left alone in Thy tabernacles, without honor and with no one to thank Thee for the gift of Thy Real Presence? Why is the world kept in the dark concerning Thee in this Most Holy Sacrament, when Thou art all that this world needs, and all that souls desire?

(*Vultus Christi* -Thursday of Adoration and Reparation for Priests)

I often think, for instance, of Mary Magdalen; hers was certainly a very enviable lot. With her tears, she bathed the feet of her Savior, she kissed them with her lips. I think of the Apostle Thomas, too. His was also an enviable lot: he touched with his finger, at least he was invited by the Lord to do so and even commanded, the adorable wounds on the glorified Body. But it seems to me that Saint John's privilege was still greater, because he leaned his head on the breast of Jesus at the Last Supper and listened to the throbbing of that adorable Heart of love and maybe saw in a vision before him all the Communions of all the ages down to the end of time.

But I am more favored than any of those, because I enjoy the happiness of receiving this dear Sacrament again and again. Daily I may lay my weary head upon my Savior's breast. No, more than that; daily I receive Him into my heart, daily I am transformed into Him so intimately that the heavenly Father, looking down upon me, sees not so much me as His well-beloved Son. 'My God and my all!' How true it is. 'My God, my only good, Thou art all mine; grant that I may be all Thine!

(*The Real Presence* - Eustace Boylan, S.J.)

You envy the opportunity of the woman who touched the vestments of Jesus, of the sinful woman who washed His feet with her tears, of the women of Galilee who had the happiness of following Him in His pilgrimages, of the Apostles and disciples who conversed with Him familiarly, of the people of the time who listened to the words of grace and salvation which came forth from His lips. You call happy those who saw Him...But, come to the altar and you will see Him, you will touch Him, you will give to Him holy kisses, you will wash Him with your tears, you will carry Him within you like Mary Most Holy.

(Attributed to Saint John Chrysostom)

Jesus inflames us in the nearness of that Holy Host. This is the enclosed garden, the place selected for Divine appointments...for holy conversations...for divine loves...

Here, at the foot of this altar, the palpitations of the heart are also supernatural, desiring the possession of God, celebrating the Mysteries of the life of the heart with Him.

Here the tongue truly occupies itself only in praising...the eyes in crying...and the heart in loving the One Who is all lovable...Here love grows and grows until it has no other wish or desire but the will of God. Here, Jesus of my soul, I love oblivion, scorn, and obscurity; and the world and worldly things are removed from my heart according to the measure that my spirit possesses You! You are the glory of my life, Eucharistic Jesus. I am happy here, consuming myself in Your presence like the candles on the altar...I languish from the love of possessing You, with an insatiable hunger for a greater union and more sacrifices.

But why is it that we feel Jesus here? Because of the emptiness of the soul, because the world is very far away, because we have no witnesses and the solitude of the heart is complete. And this is why my love grows according to the measure that I empty myself...that I humble myself...that I sink...that I lose myself in my unworthiness and in my nothingness.

(*Holy Hours* - Concepcion Carbrera de Armida)

...to the humble man the rose is redder than to the ordinary man. I say with all humility, but with complete confidence, that to the devout believer in the Real Presence, the rose is redder than to other men, the sky is of a deeper blue, the meaning of life is more profound, the light on the path more intense, and the joy which is in the heart of things more easily apprehended. For God is not only in His heaven, not only present everywhere in the inscrutable immensity of His Divine nature, but He is present in our midst in a way that grips our heart-strings, looking into our souls with His human eyes, assuaging our bruises with His human hands, loving us with His human heart, and whispering to us from the tabernacle where the little lamp glows before the Sacred Presence, 'Come to Me and I will give you rest.'

(*The Real Presence* - Eustace Boylan, S.J.)

Eucharistic adorers share Mary's life and mission of prayer at the foot of the Most Blessed Sacrament. It is the most beautiful of all missions, and it holds no perils.

(Saint Peter Julian Eymard)

As the devotion to the Sacred Heart of Jesus makes us true and faithful adorers of Jesus Christ in the most Blessed Sacrament, so it also procures for us the greatest favors. It might be said that our Lord measures the singular favors He grants herein, by the number of insults He has received; and that, there is no mystery in which He has received so many outrages, so there is none in which He fills with sweeter consolations those who neglect nothing to repair these indignities.

The motive of this holy practice being so pure and so pleasing to Jesus Christ, we need not wonder if, as He is the best and holiest of all Masters, He gives so much consolation to His faithful and grateful servants, especially at a time when He meets with so little gratitude, so little true love, in those even, who make a profession of loving Him.

(*Devotion to the Sacred Heart* - Father John Croiset, S.J.)

But anyone who would approach this gracious Sacrament while guilty of deadly sin would receive no grace from it, even though such a person would really be receiving Me as I am, wholly God, wholly human. But do you know the situation of the soul who receives the Sacrament unworthily? She is like a candle that has been doused with water and only hisses when it is brought under the fire. The flame no more than touches it but it goes out and nothing remains but smoke. Just so, this soul brings the candle she received in holy baptism and throws the water of sin over it, a water that drenches the wick of baptismal grace that is meant to bear the light. And unless she dries the wick out with the fire of true contrition by confessing her sin, she will physically receive the light when she approaches the table of the altar, but she will not receive it into her spirit.

If the soul is not disposed as she should be for so great a mystery, this true light will not graciously remain in her but will depart, leaving her more confounded, more darksome, and more deeply in sin. She will have gained nothing from this Sacrament but the hissing of remorse, not because of any defect in the light (for nothing can impair it) but because of the water it encountered in the soul, the water that so drenched her love that she could not receive this light.

(*The Dialogue* - Jesus to Saint Catherine of Siena)

They feel great tenderness and devotion who go to Jerusalem and visit the cave where the Incarnate Word was born, the hall where He was scourged, the hill of Calvary on which He died, and the sepulcher where He was buried; but how much greater ought our tenderness to be when we visit an altar on which Jesus remains in the Holy Sacrament!

(Saint Alphonsus Liguori)

'Blessed are thou among women!' O mother of God, all praise to you! You are a tabernacle of innocence and holiness - the only tabernacle worthy of Jesus.

It was you who gave to the world the Bread of Life: you had first to be the bread of life to Him before He could be the bread of Life to us...To men, weakened by sin, you gave the Bread of the Strong; to men, starved through feeding on the empty vanities of this world, you gave the Bread of Angels. Be forever praised and thanked...

(*Eucharistic Whisperings* - Father Winfrid Herbst, S.D.S.)

You consider Zacchaeus happy because Our Lord vouchsafed to enter his house and eat with him; you deem Saint John happy because he rested on the breast of our Savior at the Last Supper; and, above all, you regard Saint Joseph and the Blessed Virgin Mary so very happy because they nourished and supported Our Dear Lord. But are you not as happy as they? Are you not even happier? You do not hold Our Lord in your arms as Simeon did, but you receive Him into your heart in Holy Communion; you do not rest on the bosom of Saint John, but the Savior rests in your heart after Holy Communion; you do not nurse and support Our Lord like Saint Joseph and the Blessed Virgin, but you have a still greater happiness, for the Savior Himself nourishes you and gives Himself to you as your food. O Love! O Love! O who can understand the love of God for men!

(*The Blessed Eucharist* - Father Michael Muller, C.S.S.R.)

O my children! Our Lord is hidden there, waiting for us to come and visit Him and make our requests. See how good He is! He accommodates Himself to our weakness.

In Heaven, where we shall be glorious and triumphant, we shall see Him in all His glory. If He presented Himself before us in that glory now, we should not dare to approach Him, but He hides Himself like a person in a prison and seems to say, 'You do not see Me, but that does not matter; ask of Me all you wish and I will grant it.' He is there in the Sacrament of His love, sighing and interceding incessantly with His Father for sinners.

To what outrages does He not expose Himself, that He may remain in our midst!

He is there to console us, and therefore we ought to visit Him. How pleasing to Him is the short quarter of an hour that we steal from our occupations, from something of no consequence, to come and pray to Him, to visit Him, to console Him for all the outrages He receives! When He sees pure souls coming eagerly to Him, He smiles upon them... They come with that simplicity which pleases Him so much, to ask pardon for all sinners, for the outrages of so many ungrateful souls.

We have repeatedly received the adorable Body and the precious Blood of Jesus Christ without profit. Have we reason to be satisfied? There are many fatal causes from which this misfortune may proceed.

Each one should examine himself on this point. The general dispositions which we ought to bring to Communion are: profound humility and a sincere acknowledgment of our poverty; a certain spiritual hunger, which indicates, at the same time, the need we have of this food, and our good dispositions to profit by it; a great purity of heart, an ardent love of Jesus Christ, or at least an ardent desire of loving Him, and of accomplishing the design which He had in giving Himself to us in the Eucharist — namely, to unite us intimately to Him by a perfect conformity of heart and mind.

(Devotion to The Sacred Heart - Father John Croiset, S.J.)

If worldly people ask why you communicate so often, say it is in order to learn to love God, to purge yourself of your imperfections, to free yourself from your miseries, to console yourself in your afflictions, to support yourself in your weaknesses. Say that there are two kinds of people who should communicate often: the perfect, because being so well-disposed they would do great wrong if they did not approach the source and fountain of perfection, and the imperfect with the end of being reasonably able to inspire perfection; the strong, that they may not become weak, and the weak to become strong; the sick that they may be cured, and the healthy that they may not fall sick; and that you, imperfect, weak and sick, need to communicate often with Him who is your perfection, your strength and your doctor.

(St Francis de Sales)

But if it is true that without Christ Jesus we 'can do nothing', how much more will that be found true when it is a matter of our carrying out the action which is the holiest one of each day! To unite oneself Sacramentally to Christ Jesus in the

Eucharist is, for a created being, the highest act there can be. All human wisdom, whatever heights it may reach, is nothing in comparison with that act. We are incapable of adequately disposing ourselves in this without the help of Christ Himself. Our prayers show the reverence we have for Him, but it is He Himself who must prepare a dwelling for Himself

As the psalmist says: 'The Most High has sanctified His own tabernacle.' Let that be something we ask of Our Lord by going to visit the Sacrament of the Altar in the afternoon.

'O Christ Jesus, Word Incarnate, I want to prepare for you a dwelling within me, but I am incapable of that work. 0 Eternal Wisdom, I ask you to dispose my soul to become your temple through your infinite merits; make me be attached to you alone. I offer you my actions and my sufferings of this day, in order that you may make them pleasing to your Divine gaze, and that tomorrow I do not come before you with empty hands.'

(*Christ, The Life of the Soul* - Blessed Columba Marmion)

O Jesus, Divine Prisoner of Love, when I consider Your love and how You emptied Yourself for me, my senses deaden. You hide Your inconceivable majesty and lower Yourself to miserable me. O king of Glory, though You hide Your beauty, yet the eye of my soul rends the veil. I see the angelic choirs giving You honor without cease, and all the heavenly Powers praising You without cease, and without cease they are saying: Holy, Holy, Holy.

Oh, who will comprehend Your love and Your unfathomable mercy toward us! O Prisoner of Love, I lock up my poor heart in this tabernacle that it may adore You without cease night and day. I know of no obstacle in this adoration: and even though I be physically distant, my heart is always with You. Nothing can put a stop to my love for You. No obstacles exist for me...

(*The Divine Mercy in My Soul* – *Diary of Saint Faustina Kowalska*)

As the sanctity and merit of our actions depends on the motive and spirit with which they are actuated, the practice of the devotion to the Sacred Heart of Jesus, however holy, would be of little use, unless it were animated with the spirit and the motive which gives it all its value.

This motive, as we have said, is to repair, as far as possible, by our love, our adoration, and by every kind of homage the indignities and outrages which Jesus Christ has endured, and still daily endures, in the most Blessed Sacrament. It is in this spirit, and in these sentiments, the devotion should be practiced.

(*Devotion to the Sacred Heart* - Father John Croiset, S.J.)

... I will treasure more than anything else the Holy Sacrifice of the Mass. It is often said that it is the Mass that matters. This means that Mass is the most important thing in the world. It is very true. But I really think that sanctifying grace matters most of all. Still, where do I get that from if not through the Sacrifice of the Cross which is continued in the Sacrifice of the Mass. I am afraid. I do not think as highly of Holy Mass as I should. And this reminds me of a story I have often read about the Sacred linen in Greenland. It was in the sixteenth century. There had been a religious persecution in the island and all priests had been killed or driven out, so that for fifty years there was no Mass at all in Greenland.

After fifty years, there were still some scattered Catholics left. They used to meet every year for a Christmas celebration in a lonely house almost covered by snow. On one such night they all gathered together in the house. First, they said some prayers. Then an old man arose, went to a bureau, and took from it what used to be a white cloth, like a big, square napkin. Now it was yellow with age and tattered. It was a corporal, that linen cloth on which, during Holy Mass, rest the Body and Blood of Christ. The old man said: 'Brethren, fifty years ago Mass was last said in this country. I served that last Mass. Let us kneel down and thank God for this precious relic, on which rested the Body and Blood of Jesus. And let us pray that God may send us priests to offer the Holy Sacrifice in our midst again.'

Tears streamed from all eyes as they knelt to pray. And all around me there are now so many churches and so many Masses are being offered. I do not think I value enough the chances that I have to assist at Holy Mass. Where there is a persecution and hearing Mass is forbidden under pain of torture or death, good Catholics nevertheless go to Mass, even if it is in caves under the ground.

Those good people in Greenland knelt down and thanked God for that precious Sacred linen. How happy and how devout they would have been if they could have bowed down before Jesus Himself in the Blessed Sacrament! And I am often so careless and thoughtless in my genuflections and in my way of kneeling or sitting or standing in the presence of my Eucharistic Savior. And it seems that the more I have to do around the Blessed Sacrament, the more like a pagan I become.

(*The Way to God* - Father Winfrid Herbst, S.D.S.)

Ah, if we had the eyes of Angels with which to see our Lord Jesus Christ who is here present on this altar and who is looking at us, how we should love Him! We should never more wish to part from Him; we should wish to remain always at His feet. It would be a foretaste of Heaven. All else would become insipid to us. But see, it is faith we lack. We are poor blind people; we have a mist before our eyes. Faith alone can dispel this mist.

(*The Holy Eucharist Our All* - Father Lukas Etlin, O.S.B., quoting Saint John Vianney)

O my beloved Jesus, O God, who has loved me with love exceeding! What more can You do to make Yourself loved by ungrateful people? If we loved You, all the churches would be continually filled with people prostrate on the ground adoring and thanking You, burning with love for You, and seeing You with the eyes of faith, hidden in a tabernacle. But no, we are forgetful of You and Your love. We are ready enough to try to win the favor of a person from whom we hope for some miserable advantage, while we leave You, Lord, abandoned and alone. If only by my devotion I could make reparation for such ingratitude! I am sorry that I have also been careless and ungrateful.

In the future, I will change my ways, I will devote myself to Your service as much as possible. Inflame me with Your holy love, so that from this day forward I may live only to love and to please You. You deserve the love of all hearts. If at one time I have despised You, I now desire nothing but to love You. O my Jesus, You are my love and my only good, 'my God and my All'.

(*Meditations on the Eucharist* - Saint Alphonsus Liguori)

He makes it ever clearer to me that He wants me to burn with love for Him in devotion to the Blessed Sacrament. Every time I receive Him I must feel renewed that longing which stirs within me to live for Jesus only and to obtain the grace of preservation from so many sins which I should certainly commit if He did not come to my help. How can I remain deaf to His invitation?

(Attributed to Cardinal Angelo Roncalli (Pope John XXIII)

My Jesus in the Blessed Sacrament, how can I ever express the sympathy and sorrow which should be expressed for the unbelievable foolishness which we show in our daily neglect of You...You offer us so much in the Mass and in Holy Communion, yet we do so little to deserve Your generosity and love. Lord place my heart in Yours for a moment and inflame it with the fire of Your love. Let me grow in appreciation of Holy Communion, so that I may come to You more often...

(*The Sacrifice of the Mass* - Cardinal Giovanni Bona)

The great test of humility is the pain of not receiving love for love, and that too Thou dost bear. In this Sacrament, Thou dost live entirely for me. Thine unbounded love urges the desire to unite Thyself with me in Holy Communion. Thou dost long to enrich me with Thy blessings and gladden my soul. And yet what do I give Thee in return? What do so many of us Catholics do to return love for love? How many of us pay scant attention to Thine invitation! How many of us fail to receive Thee frequently in Holy Communion! Too often are we cold and ungrateful, unmindful of Thy love, half-hearted or even irreverent at Mass and Holy Communion! Thou dost patiently bear with this indifference. Despite our ingratitude, Thou dost continue to grant us countless blessings and thus teach us the noblest kind of humility: to love even when love is not returned; to embrace even humiliations.

(*A Novena of Holy Communions* - Father Lawrence G. Lovasik, S.V.D.)

Reflecting, before Holy Communion, on the essential, intimate association of the Holy Spirit with the central mystery of our Catholic Faith, we will beg Him to remove far from us whatever would impede our reception of the fullness of the grace of this Sacrament. We will do more. With an ardor that dilates our hearts with exquisite joy, we will constrain Him to ennoble our thoughts and desires so that we may embrace Christ with a faith that moves mountains, and with a love supremely sacrificial. Then will we glorify our hidden God, and our souls will be His home until the shadows flee away, and we return with the garnered fruits of infinite, eternal love, to contemplate forever, the inexhaustible beauty that we adored under the Eucharistic veil.

(*Transforming Your Life Through the Eucharist* - Father John A. Kane)

Nothing afflicts the Heart of Jesus so much as to see all His sufferings of no avail to so many.

(Saint John Vianney)

The particular object of this devotion [to the Sacred Heart] is the immense love of the Son of God, which has induced Him to die for us, and to give Himself wholly to us in the Adorable Sacrament of the Altar, and this, although He foresaw all the ingratitude and outrages which He was to meet within this state of a victim immolated till the end of ages; preferring rather to expose himself daily to the insults and contempt of mankind, than to fail in showing us, by the greatest of all wonders, to what an excess He loves us.

This is what has enkindled the piety and zeal of many. Reflecting on the little gratitude that is shown for such an excess of love, the little love that is felt for Jesus Christ, and the little value that is set upon His love for us, they have been unable to endure to see Him daily so ill-treated, without protesting to Him their just grief and their excessive desire to repair, as far as they can, so much ingratitude and contempt, by their ardent love, by their profound respect, and by every sort of homage in their power. It is with this intention that certain days in the year have been chosen in order to make a more special recognition of the excessive love of Jesus Christ for us in the adorable Sacrament; and at the same time, to make Him some reparation of honor for all the indignities and all the contempt which He has received, and still receives daily, in this mystery of love.

And certainly, this grief at the sight of the little love shown to Jesus Christ in this adorable mystery, this intense sorrow at seeing Him so ill-treated, these practices of devotion which are suggested by love alone, and which have no other aim but to repair, as far as possible, the outrages He there endures, are, without doubt, real proofs of an ardent love for Jesus Christ, and visible signs of a just gratitude.

(*Devotion to the Sacred Heart* – Father John Croiset, S.J.)

In the presence of Jesus in the Blessed Sacrament I invariably find something that the world always hides from me, namely, knowledge of self. In the light of the Holy Eucharist all my faults and failings and all my sins, past and present, become clear to me; and then from the very depths of my heart there wells up a cleansing, purifying font of sorrow. Oh, how poor and miserable I appear to myself when in the presence of Jesus! And yet how sweet and salutary are the tears that I shed at the sight of transgressions!

If I cannot find it here, then where in the world can I find it – a little patch of earth, I mean, one to be watered by my tears so that thereon the tender blossoms of hope may germ and grow? Who, if not Jesus, can say to me, 'Go in peace, thy sins are forgiven thee'?

(*Eucharistic Whisperings* - Father Winfrid Herbst, S.D.S.)

Christmas night rocked Heaven. Angels were aghast at the Incarnation. But Holy Thursday night struck them dumb. That God should become a Babe in swaddling clothes was cause for overwhelming surprise; but that God should bury Himself in Bread and become the very Food of man dazzled and stupefied the nine choirs of Heaven's court. And yet, great as was God's action, they were not completely bewildered by it. No! It took man's reaction to do that! Heaven was not completely bewildered until it saw man's coldness to God's condescension.

Bethlehem closed doors – but Bethlehem did not really know who Joseph was or whom Mary tabernacled. Roman soldiers scourged Christ and hammered Him to a Cross while High priests howled and frenzied Jews mocked; but none of these fully understood what they did or who He was. But you! – you have made profession after profession of your belief. You say that you know that God is on your altars; that He is there with His Body and His Blood, His soul and Divinity under the guise of Bread and the appearances of Wine. You proclaim to believe that God is Emmanuel – God with us – yet, you leave Him alone!...

[Seraphim] do not understand men and women and even growing children who say that they want life and love, and then deliberately neglect the only Food and Drink that will give them life and love, preserve them in life and love, and augment their lives and their loves! Heaven cannot understand your neglect of Christ in the Holy Eucharist. Can you?

(A Trappist Asks Do You Want Life and Love?)

O dear Lord, if my faith were more vivid, I would see that this happiness is virtually mine. I can speak to You here, knowing that You are close to me, that You are looking at me, that You are listening to me, just as You did when among those friends who pressed You here on earth, gaining strength of body and soul from Your gracious Presence.

(An Hour with Our Savior)

To cast fire upon the earth—that is my mission! And how I wish it were already blazing fiercely! Nothing in the world can set hearts ablaze with love for God like the Blessed Sacrament. That is why this Divine Bread has been pictured as a furnace of love. Saint Catherine of Siena saw far-reaching flames coming from this furnace of love and spreading throughout the world. Seeing this, Catherine simply could not understand how so many people could live without loving God.

My Lord, set me on fire with love for you. Let me think of nothing, crave for nothing, yearn for nothing, search for nothing, but you. How I wish to be caught up in this scorching fire of love! How I wish it would consume every obstacle that blocks my path toward you! Make my love for you grow stronger each day of my life.

(Saint Alphonsus Liguori - Missionaries of the Blessed Sacrament)

We cannot separate our lives from the Eucharist; the moment we do, something breaks. People ask, 'Where do the sisters get the joy and energy to do what they are doing?' The Eucharist involves more than just receiving; it also involves satisfying the hunger of Christ. He says, 'Come to Me.' He is hungry for souls. Nowhere does the Gospel say: 'Go away,' but always 'Come to Me.'

Our lives must be woven around the Eucharist. Ask Jesus to be with you, to work with you that you may be able to pray the work. You must really be sure that you have received Jesus. After that, you cannot give your tongue, your thoughts, or your heart to bitterness.

(Saint Teresa of Calcutta)

The Eucharistic Heart in the Host draws me more and more. If I merely pass near the chapel, I feel an irresistible force inviting me in. Close to the tabernacle, I experience an indefinable joy. When the Blessed Sacrament is exposed, I feel totally taken over, paralyzed, by this gentle Eucharistic Heart. When I leave the chapel, I have to tear myself away from the Divine Prisoner. Yet, I never cease to live in Him; all this takes place in the Heart of the Most Blessed Trinity, an immense distance from the earth; but Jesus wants me to enjoy Him in his Eucharist and to grieve when I am far from His consecrated Host?

(Blessed Dina Belanger)

Try every morning, when you have the joy of receiving Communion, to ask our Lord to remain with you all day in your soul...When I think now of how I used to be envious of Mary Magdalene for having had Jesus in her home so often, for having heard Him, I'm ashamed, since He has not abandoned this world. He's present in the Tabernacle. I gaze upon Him in faith, and hear Him.

(Saint Teresa of the Andes)

I believe everything the Church teaches about the Holy Eucharist. I believe, even if I do not understand, even if I do not see. I know that those are blessed who do not see and yet believe. The Savior said so. It reminds me of the story that is told about Saint Louis IX of France. One day a miracle took place in a nearby church. Someone came rushing to the King and said: 'Hurry, Your Majesty! Jesus has appeared in the

Host in human figure during Mass.' But the King did not hurry. He did not even go. He said: 'Let those go to see the miracle who have any doubt about the Real Presence. I need no miracle. I believe.

(*The Way to God* - Father Winfrid Herbst, S.D.S.)

I never go up into the pulpit without seeking to move [souls] to love of the Divine Eucharist, and I often recommend the visit to the Blessed Sacrament. Given that example speaks louder than words, I go habitually to recite Vespers, Compline, and later, Matins and Lauds before the Blessed Sacrament in the cathedral, and at nightfall I make a half-hour's meditation there. The Lord will, I hope, bless these efforts, by stirring up in a greater number of souls the desire to visit the Blessed Sacrament. I say this only for you, so that your heart may be consoled by it. Persevere in your holy undertaking, in the midst of difficulties and contradictions. The railway cars are overflowing with travelers while the avenues leading to churches where the Holy Eucharist resides are deserted. This is truly the hidden and unknown God. Apply yourself to making Him known, praised, loved, blessed and welcomed.

(November 1855 letter from the Bishop of Lucon to Virginie Danion)

No wonder Angels frown. Jesus Christ so loved man that He died for him; and 'greater love than this no man has!' Ah, Jesus Christ is God and he has a greater love for man than man's love. He gave man proof of love by dying; He gives God's proof by living. Jesus Christ died; He arose from the dead; He ascended into heaven; and yet, He would not leave the earth! No. He loves man too much! He must be near man. That is love's way. Nearness is not enough; love craves union! So Jesus Christ became Food and Drink that He might live in man and man might live in Him. The Divine Beggar has beggared Himself. More, He cannot do...

(A Trappist Asks Do You Want Life and Love?)

We need a blood transfusion...There must be communication, union, between the Heart of Jesus and your heart – our heart – so that His Divine blood will flow into us until little by little our blood is replaced by His. When this union, this total fusion between our will and His will takes place, then, to put it briefly, our will is replaced with the will of Jesus; our feelings are replaced with the feelings of Jesus. We live in Jesus – this is love! We are lost in Jesus. It is no longer I who think, it is no longer I who feel; it is no longer I who act. It is Jesus in me! It is Christ who lives in me!

(Blessed James Alberione as quoted by Sr. Marie Paul Curley, fsp on *Windows to the Soul Blog*)

There are prayerful steps we can take, in the silence of Eucharistic Adoration, to hear the Lord's voice. We can begin by thanking God for His presence, and by asking Him to help us to know Him, and to love Him. We can acknowledge our distractions, and ask the Lord to give us the gift of silence. And, through Scripture, or the mysteries of the rosary, through some other spiritual practice or reading, or through simple contemplation of God's goodness, we can begin to hear the Lord's voice. We can share our hearts with the Lord, and ask Him to fill our minds, our imaginations, and our hearts with His presence.

God speaks to us when He is present before us in the Eucharist. We need only learn His language: we need only dare to kneel humbly before the Lord and, with trust in God, begin a dialogue of silence—intimate, powerful, and real.

(Pastoral Letter on Adoration of the Most Holy Eucharist - Bishop James Conley)

O my daughter! Would that the believers in the holy Catholic faith opened their hardened and stony hearts in order to attain to a true understanding of the Sacred and mysterious blessing of the Holy Eucharist!

If they would only detach themselves, root out and reject their earthly inclinations, and, restraining their passions, apply themselves with living faith to study by the Divine light their great happiness in thus possessing their eternal God in the Holy Sacrament and in being able, by its reception and constant intercourse, to participate in the full effects of this heavenly manna!

If they would only worthily esteem this precious gift, begin to taste its sweetness, and share in the hidden power of their omnipotent God! Then nothing would ever be wanting to them in their exile.

In this, the happy age of the law of grace, mortals have no reason to complain of their weakness and their passions; since in this Bread of heaven they have at hand strength and health. It matters not that they are tempted and persecuted by the demon; for by receiving this Sacrament frequently they are able to overcome him gloriously. The faithful are themselves to blame for all their poverty and labors, since they pay no attention to this Divine mystery, nor avail themselves of the Divine powers, thus placed at their disposal by my most Holy Son...

Lucifer and his demons have such a fear of the most holy Eucharist, that to approach it, causes them more torments than to remain in hell itself. Although they do enter churches in order to tempt souls, they enter them with aversion, forcing themselves to endure cruel pains in the hope of destroying a soul and drawing it into sin, especially in the holy places and in the presence of the Holy Eucharist.

(The Mystical City of God - words of Our Lady to Blessed Mary of Agreda)

Of all the benefits we have received from Jesus Christ, we cannot doubt that the Blessed Eucharist is one of the greatest; and even the greater part of the blessings we daily receive, are derived from the same source.

But who thinks of often thanking Jesus Christ for this great benefit? Who returns thanks to this loving Savior, Who, in abolishing all the other sacrifices, has left us a Victim that cannot but be pleasing to God, an offering equal to all the other benefits we have received from Him, and to those that we may ask of Him; a Host capable of cancelling all the sins of men; a Host which is truly a sovereign remedy for all kinds of evil; a tree of life that has power to communicate to us, not only health, but even immortality?

So sinful a forgetfulness, such enormous ingratitude, touched the Heart of a Man-God, and shall it not move mine, even when I myself am of the number of these ungrateful wretches?

(Devotion to the Sacred Heart - Father John Croiset, S.J.)

And to You, O God of my soul, to You I refuse the very alms of a prayer, of an act of contrition, of a purpose of amendment!...I dare to refuse You one quarter of an hour's adoration, the hearing of Holy Mass, the reception of Holy Communion...How lamentably considerate I am as regards my unruly passions; only in Your regard am I inconsiderate and hard of heart!

(*Eucharistic Whisperings* - Father Winfrid Herbst, S.D.S.)

Christ is God-made-man: He comes to dwell among us. This earth has borne His imprint and we walk on it, each step of ours an adventure in faith, love, and hope. How can we not love this earth upon which He walked? How can we not get from it the strength that the imprints of His feet have left there? Because, you know, His footprints are still in its dust, and His blood is still mixed with it. How can we enter anyplace where the Blessed Sacrament reposes, and not be filled with joy, and renewed in hope in strength? Yes, He has come! He will be coming again in the Parousia, but He is with us now! He is Emmanuel ('God with us').

(Servant of God Catherine Doherty)

'Where dost Thou live?' We know the answer in theory. He [Jesus] dwells in the Eucharist. But, in practice, do we know it? All that requires a search, an extra effort, maybe an hour to find out. That is why in answer to their question, He answered: 'Come and see.' The 'come' is a visit; to 'see' is to enjoy. The first words that fell from the lips of Him Who is the Bread of Life were an invitation to seek greater union with Him.

(Venerable Fulton J. Sheen)

The peace of soul that is ours in our moments of adoration is a blissful exaltation above the turmoil of time, an anticipation of the eternal peace of Heaven. Our union with the Eucharistic worshipers, the myriad hosts of angels that surround the tabernacle, adoring in Heaven as they gaze forever on His soul-stirring Divinity, humbly prostrate before Him in His Sacramental lowliness as He hides the beauty that would overwhelm us - what is this but paradise on earth?

Thus raised above the visible, we can forego its claims and honor Christ for His own dear sake. We can compensate for the irreverence of those who believe, but do not realize, the mystery of His Real Presence, and for the profanations of those who absolutely deny it. If we love Christ, we will gladly spend ourselves trying to repair the dishonor which He so patiently endures in the Sacrament of His love. The conscious recognition of what He suffers will help us to increase our love of Him.

Our reparation does not remove the injuries, nor do we absolve the offenders by offering our love as compensation for their want of love. But heart speaking to heart in understanding sympathy gives to the heart's desires an additional value...

(Transforming Your Life through the Eucharist - Father John A. Kane)

Why dilute your love in an unceasing flow of words? Why destroy the charm of intimate communings with Him by childish loquacity? May the silence of the Eucharist teach you silent recollection! But, while your lips are still, let your eyes speak. Yes, tell it all to Jesus with a long gaze full of adoration, love, and pleading. Put all your tenderness in that look, all your desires, your sorrows, your disillusions - in a word, your whole soul. Stir up your faith and seek the eyes of Jesus through the Eucharistic veils. May His gaze and yours meet, be united, and form together one and the same light and one and the same fire of love. Why do you look for more? Ask Him only to deign to look upon you. Tell Him with entire confidence: 'Look upon me and have mercy on me' (Ps 118:132). Remembering that, as soon as Jesus had looked on that young man who came to Him, He loved him, fear not to tell Him also: 'Look upon me and ... love me!'

(*The Holy Eucharist* - Jose Guadalupe Trevino)

God has blessed our Churches with His Real Presence where He can be worshiped, adored and loved, where He changes, heals and comforts the hearts and souls (and sometimes bodies) of many. Yet few come to keep Him company or to make reparation to Him for those who do not believe in Him. Where are the courageous prayer warriors willing to get up in the early morning hours to be with Him while the rest of us sleep? How sad and lonely is Our Lord – so intimately present among us but ignored by the majority of people claiming to love Him.

(*I Thirst For Your Love*)

Jesus is present and lives in our midst in the Eucharist. Let us listen to Him for He is Truth. Let us look at Him, for He is the face of the Father. Let us love Him, for He is love giving Himself to His creatures. He comes to our souls so that it might disappear in Him and become Divine. What union, however great, can compare to this?

(*Prayers for Eucharistic Adoration* - Saint Teresa of the Andes)

In Your dear Presence I humbly kneel, sweet Savior mine; and while I contemplate Your goodness to me I bewail my base ingratitude towards You. My Jesus, mercy…and grace!

Oh…I am astonished at my boldness, when I consider that I am here in Your very Presence, in the Presence of the omnipotent God! Were not my proper place in deepest hell, after all that I have done against You?…but instead of that I linger in Your consoling Presence here, delighting in the tender familiarities of Your boundless love!…It is still permitted me peacefully to repose in the fragrant atmosphere of prayer; I am still tolerated among the good. Unto the hermits of the desert You gave to drink water from the rock-bound spring; and to eat, the herbs and roots of the earth. But to me You give the adorable Food of Your Flesh and Blood. How can I but marvel?

I acknowledge it, my Jesus: it is bold of me to linger here in the delicious abundance of Your graces. But, surely, since You do not spurn my poor, miserable self, neither will You reject my heartfelt sorrow.

(*Eucharistic Whisperings* - Father Winfrid Herbst, S.D.S.)

Go to our Lord just as you are. Make a simple meditation. Exhaust your own fund of piety and love before you make use of books. Love the inexhaustible book of humility and charity. However, it is well to take with you a pious book, in order to recall your thoughts when your mind wanders or when your senses are dull.

Remember that our good Master prefers the poverty of our heart to the most sublime thoughts and affections borrowed from others. Understand well that our Lord desires our own heart, and not that of others. He wants the thought and the prayer of your heart as a natural expression of love for Him.

To be unwilling to go to our Lord with one's misery and one's humiliating poverty, is often the fruits of subtle self-love, of restlessness or tepidity, and yet that misery and poverty are what our Lord prefers to every other gift. He loves it. He blesses it.

(*My Eucharistic Day – Rules and Practices* - Saint Peter Julian Eymard)

Poor, pitiable sinners. Do not turn away from Me...Day and night I am on watch for you in the tabernacle. I will not reproach you...I will not cast your sins in your face...But I will wash them in My blood and My wounds. No need to be afraid...Come to Me...If you only knew how dearly I love you.

(*The Way of Divine Love* - Jesus to Sister Josefa Menendez)

Saint Joseph believed unhesitatingly in the mystery of the Incarnation, in the fruitful virginity and the divine maternity of Mary. He believed without seeing the miracles that were to fill Judea with His glory and renown of His holy name.

We too should recognize Jesus in the frail Host that is offered to us at the altar. Here He is even smaller than at Bethlehem, more hidden than in Joseph's workshop. Still it is He.

(Bishop Peter Anastasius Pichenot)

I remain unknown. I am left alone. Even those who claim to profess the mystery of my Real Presence in the Sacrament of the Altar forsake Me. I am treated with a terrible indifference, with coldness, and with a lack of respect that causes the angels to weep because they cannot offer Me reparation for the coldness and indifference of human hearts. Only men can make reparation for men. What is lacking is the loving response of a human heart to My Eucharistic Heart, pierced, alive and beating in the Sacrament of the Altar. Only a human heart can make reparation for a human heart. For this reason, the angels are sorrowful.

Our wonderful Father and Pope, Pius X, the Pope of Frequent Communion, was also the Pope of the interior life. 'Re-establish all things in Christ' was the first thing he had to say, above all to active workers. It summarizes the program of an apostle who lives on the Eucharist and who sees that the Church will gain successes only in proportion as souls make progress in the Eucharistic life.

So many enterprises in our time, and yet so often fruitless: why is it that they have not put society back on its feet? Let us admit it once again: they can be counted in far greater numbers than in preceding ages, and yet they have been unable to check the frightful ravages of impiety in the field of family life. Why? Because they are not firmly enough based on the interior life, the Eucharistic life, the liturgical life, full and properly understood.

(*The Soul of the Apostolate* - Jean-Baptiste Chautard, O.C.S.O.)

Aside from the Blessed Virgin, Saint Joseph was the first and most perfect adorer of our Lord. Among the graces which Jesus gave to His foster-father — and He flooded him with graces attached to every one of His mysteries — is that special to an adorer of the Blessed Sacrament. That is the one we must ask of Saint Joseph. Have confidence, strong confidence in him. Take him as the patron and the model of your life of adoration.

(Saint Peter Julian Eymard)

Man should tremble, the world should quake, all Heaven should be deeply moved when the Son of God appears on the altar in the hands of the priest.

(Saint Francis of Assisi)

Whenever we are shaken by the sight of evil spreading in the universe…we should not forget that such unleashing of the forces of sin is overcome by the saving power of Christ. Whenever the words of consecration are uttered in the Mass and the Body and Blood of Christ become present in the act of the sacrifice, the triumph of love over hatred, of holiness over sin, is also present. Every Eucharistic Celebration is stronger than all the evil in the universe…

(Saint John Paul II)

The adoration and the praise they offer Me is angelic. It is the expression of the perfections I have placed in their angelic nature. Without ever dying, they immolate themselves before Me in the tabernacles where I dwell on earth by lowering themselves in the most humble adoration and by placing all their angelic perfections – their beauty, their strength, their intelligence – beneath My feet. The angels are like living flames who burn in My Eucharistic Presence, without ever being consumed. Yet for all of this, My angels cannot replace a single human heart in My Presence. What I look for from men, what I wait for, above all from my priests, My angels cannot give Me.

(In Sinu Jesu – When Heart Speaks to Heart – The Journal of a Priest)

The most powerful thing we can do on this earth with our time is to spend it in Eucharistic Adoration. Nothing can do more to change the world, to bring about peace, to convert hearts, to make reparation for the many evils committed.

Spending time in prayer may seem, on the outside, to be a passive thing; however, it is anything but! Our world is in desperate need of hope, of renewal, of a 'turning back' to the things of God. By visiting our Lord in the Blessed Sacrament, we take up the best weapon for the battles of our age and contribute to the healing of our culture.

(Manual for Eucharistic Adoration)

People come to Me for different reasons. Some come only on Sundays and holy days, through a sense of obligation. Either they do not want to lose Heaven, or they desire My help in their daily life. Then there are those who come to Me through mere habit. They act automatically, without any particular devotion to Me. There, are, however, a certain number who come to Me for the best reason. They come because they are glad to be near Me. These people please Me best of all. They receive many extra graces which are not granted to the others.

(My Daily Bread - Father Anthony J. Paone, S.J.)

O Jesus hidden God, I come before You, earnestly imploring that You would enliven my faith so that I may realize what Your Presence on this altar means. I believe with all my heart and soul that You are here, but without Your special grace my faith is dull, and moves me not as it ought to love You. I picture You as You did appear to Your disciples and friends on earth, and I think how sweet it would have been to kneel at Your Sacred feet, to kiss your Sacred hands, to tell You all my wants, my troubles, and my failings. How sweet it would have been even to linger near You, hoping for a look from Your compassionate eyes – one glance from which left Peter heartbroken for his fault against You!

(An Hour with Our Savior)

Now write for My souls: I want to tell them of the poignant sorrow which filled My heart at the Last Supper. If it was bliss for Me to think of those to whom I should be both Companion and Heavenly Food, of all those would surround

Me to the end of time with adoration, reparation and love...this in no wise diminished My grief at the many who leave Me deserted in My tabernacle and who would not even believe in My Real Presence...Sacrileges and outrages, and all the nameless abominations to be committed against Me passed before My eyes...

It is love for souls that keeps Me a prisoner in the Blessed Sacrament, I stay there that all may come and find the comfort they need in the tenderest of Hearts, the best of Fathers, the most faithful of Friends, who will never abandon them. The Holy Eucharist is the invention of Love...Yet how few souls correspond to that love which spends and consumes itself for them.

(The Way of Divine Love - Sister Josefa Menendez)

One day, when I was assisting at the Holy Sacrifice, I saw an immense number of Holy Angels descend and gather around the altar, contemplating the priest. They sang heavenly canticles that ravished my heart; Heaven itself seemed to be contemplating the great Sacrifice. And yet we poor blind and miserable creatures assist at Mass with so little love, relish and respect.

(All About Angels - St Bridget)

Here, it is so quiet, Lord. I love the quiet. It helps me absorb the idea that You are here with me, that You and I are visiting. Sometimes it seems so noisy away from here that I can't find a still place to even try to seek You out. You are elusive in the noise!

Still, I can hear the climate control systems of the building. I can hear the distant sounds of cars, sirens, playing children, barking dogs. These sounds are worldly background. In Your human form, you experienced all these noises, Lord. You know of the distinctions.

At moments like this, I can even hear my heart beating. I can hear each time I inhale and exhale. Do you breathe in Your glorified body? Do you breathe with me, Lord? Does Your Sacred Heart actually beat? Can our hearts actually beat together, in rhythm with each other?

I listen for the glory of You, our Creator, in the muted sounds surrounding me. Are You in the usual sounds around us? Are You even in my breathing and beating heart? Are You in the thoughts that pass through my mind? I want You to completely fill every thought I have and everything I am. I want to detect Your presence with my senses.

Here, it is easy to think of You, to spill my heart to You. Here the noises are not invasive. But at home, at work, in the stores, in the crowds, the sounds that block my thoughts of You are deafening.

I am comforted here in Your quiet peace. I can more easily perceive Your love here than in the midst of the world's distractions. Come home with me, Lord.

(An Hour With Jesus)

If only we could comprehend the nearness of God, the incomparable grace of having Jesus for our companion in exile. He is so near that when He blesses us, the shadow of His Divine hand hovers over us.

What does He seek? A relief from His sorrows and for that He begs the love of our hearts. Let Him rest then, let Him

pour the sorrows of His soul into ours, we who want Him with a burning love of reparation
.

From the depths of the tabernacle, His lips still wet with the gall of our ingratitude, He calls by name those who have come during this Holy Hour to weep over all the people who disregard His mercies. How great is the sorrow that torments Him! But greater still, infinitely stronger, is the love which tortures Him...

Jesus: For a long time I have waited for you, well beloved soul, to tell you of the love that consumes Me. I bless you because you have at last taken pity on your God in His loneliness. Tell me that My Heart has conquered yours. Assure Me that now you really love Me. You who are but dust and nothingness, have often left Me to seek pleasure and enjoyment, while I your God, to save you, left the angels, left heaven, and after thirty-three years of suffering died as a criminal on a cross. Despite that, you broke the bonds that united you to Me and freed yourself from My arms which upheld you, and you preferred the deadly attractions of sin to Me. Do you remember?

How could you love such a sad liberty, especially since I have forged chains to bind Me to your ungrateful heart. Where is your gratitude? And yet I forgive you, but from now on be Mine forever, entirely Mine in a spirit of gratitude and reparation.

(*Twenty Holy Hours* - Rev. Mateo Crawley-Boevey, SS.CC.)

How many knocks did your conversion cost Me?...How many times, my dear soul, did you laugh, and I was lamenting this with sighs and tears right next to you...Your resisted Me with haughtiness, and I insisted humbly with incomparable motivation…And when once You did come to open your heart, did you not experience My enthusiasm and rejoicing?

And today, what can you say?…Have I never cried at the door of your heart?…Have I not had to await humbly – and with the patience of God, and with pearls in My hands…and amidst the noise of your pride – for you to hear Me…What have I done for you except benefit you?…What am I asking for except that which should be Mine, that is, your heart – but a clean…pure…open…loving…generous…and sacrificed heart? Is this how you give it to Me?

(*Holy Hours* - Concepcion Cabrera de Armida)

Dear Jesus, what do you say about this soldier who is so cowardly and so imperfect? Forgive me. The next time I'll be better. I'll throw myself into that immense ocean of the love of your Heart, to lose myself in It like a drop of water in the ocean and to abase my littleness in the greatness of Your mercy.

(Saint Teresa of the Andes)

When communicating with Christ in your heart - the partaking of Living Bread - remember what Our Lady must have felt when the Spirit overpowered her and she, who was full of grace, became full with the body of Jesus. The Spirit was so strong in her that she immediately rose in haste to go and serve. Each Holy Communion, each breaking of the Bread of Life, each sharing should produce in us the same, for it is the same Jesus who came to Mary and was made flesh. We, too, should be in haste to give this life of Jesus…

(Saint Teresa of Calcutta)

But we must remember that, however great and ineffable is all that our Lord has done for our salvation, the love which has led Him to do it is still greater than all, because it is infinite — and as if this love could not be satisfied, so long as there remained a miracle it had not wrought, He institutes the adorable Sacrament of the Altar, the sum of all His wonders.

He truly lives with us until the end of the world. He gives Himself to us, under the appearances of bread and wine. He makes His flesh and blood the nourishment of our souls, in order to unite Himself more closely to us, or rather to unite us more closely to Him. Can we then be possessed of reason, and not be deeply moved at the mere recital of this marvel? Can we still retain any feeling of humanity, and not be all inflamed with love for Jesus Christ, at the sight of such a benefit?

A God feels tenderness for man, takes delight in him, and is solicitous about him! A God desires to unite Himself to us, and desires it to such an extent as to annihilate and immolate Himself daily, and to wish that we should feed upon Him every day, without being in the least changed, either by the indifference, the disgust, or the contempt of those who never receive Him, or by the coldness and the faults of those who receive Him often!

(*Devotion to The Sacred Heart* - Father John Croiset, S.J.)

To each of us He says from the tabernacle: 'Stay you here, and watch with Me...Could you not watch one hour with Me?' Or if not one hour, one quarter?

Stay with Me because I am going to offer My morning sacrifice, and men are too busy to assist at the oblation of Myself for them.

Stay with Me for a few moments at midday, when the glare of the world and its rush and its din are fiercest. Turn off the crowded pavement into the quiet church, 'Come apart...and rest a little.'

Stay with Me because it is towards evening and the day is now far spent. There will be no more visitors for Me today, none through the long hours of the night. Stay with Me because it is towards evening.

(*Coram Sanctissimo* - Mother Mary Loyola)

Do grant, oh my God, that when my lips approach Yours to kiss You, I may taste the gall that was given to You; when my shoulders lean against Yours, make me feel Your scourging; when my flesh is united with Yours, in the Holy Eucharist, make me feel Your passion; when my head comes near Yours, make me feel Your thorns; when my heart is close to Yours, make me feel Your spear.

(Saint Gemma Galgani)

I adore You, Lord and Creator, hidden in the Most Blessed Sacrament. I adore You for all the works of Your hands, that reveal to me so much wisdom, goodness and mercy, O Lord. You have spread so much beauty over the earth and it tells me about Your beauty, even though these beautiful things are but a faint reflection of You, incomprehensible Beauty. And although You have hidden Yourself and concealed your beauty, my eye, enlightened by faith, reaches You and my soul recognizes its Creator, its Highest Good, and my heart is completely immersed in prayer of adoration.

(*The Divine Mercy in My Soul* – Diary of Saint Faustina Kowalska)

Go and find Him when your patience and strength run out and you feel alone and helpless. Jesus is waiting for you in the chapel. Say to Him, 'Jesus, you know exactly what is going on. You are all I have, and you know all things. Come to my help.' And then go, and don't worry about how you are going to manage. That you have told God about it is enough. He has a good memory.

(Saint Jeanne Jugan)

Now listen, my Jesus! You have decided to continue Your Eucharistic mendicant-life, so I must earnestly implore You to remain with me always, ever to be at the door of my heart! Only rap, and I will always open to You; only ask, and You shall always receive! I will always give You, whatsoever You want; thoughts, words, desires, deeds of virtue, sacrifices, tears, penances – everything, everything, even my life. But there is one condition, my Jesus; I would so like to burn with love for You in the Blessed Sacrament that my love – that my love would know no bounds!

(*Eucharistic Whisperings* - Father Winfrid Herbst, S.D.S.)

O Jesus, hidden God, more friendly than a brother, I believe most firmly that You are present, a few feet only from where I kneel.

You are behind that little wall, listening to every word of confidence and love, and thanksgiving, and praise. Listening when my heart is free to pour itself out to You as the brook to the river in the days of spring. Listening more tenderly when the stream is ice-bound; when I kneel before You troubled, wearied, anxious about many things – about many souls perhaps – yet dry and hard, without a word to say.

Make my heart so perfectly at ease with You, O Lord, that it may be able to turn to You even in its coldness and inertness; to confide to You naturally all that most intimately concerns it; to be content with this, when discontented with all else, with self-most of all – that You know all men and need not that any should give testimony of man, for You know what is in man.

(*Coram Santissimo* - Mother Mary Loyola from)

Whenever I go to the chapel, I put myself in the presence of our good Lord, and I say to Him, 'Lord, I am here. Tell me what You would have me to do?...And then, I tell God everything that is in my heart. I tell him about my pains and my joys, and then I listen. If you listen, God will also speak to you, for with the good Lord, you have to both speak and listen. God always speaks to you when you approach Him plainly and simply.

(Saint Catherine Laboure)

He [Jesus] begs for one little word of kindly considerate greeting when I pass by a church...for a short ejaculatory prayer from time to time...for at least one loving aspiration when the bells ring out from the church towers...for a thought, one only thought, when I am alone. A word surely...at least a word I would not even refuse the most despicable criminal. But for Jesus?... Have I a word for Jesus? ...How many?

Into this Sacred Heart, Which is open to us, we must enter. In this Sacred Heart we must learn to pray, to thank God, to praise Him, to annihilate ourselves in His presence, but above all, to love Him. What wonders does not Jesus Christ work during these precious moments in a pure soul, in a soul that really loves Him. The mere thought of this Divine Heart fills us, at that time, with extraordinary devotion.

If Jesus Christ, in coming to us, gives us sensible marks of His presence, as is generally the case with those who have a tender devotion to His Sacred Heart, let us profit by these precious moments, let us preserve great interior recollection, let us listen to our Lord, let us allow grace to work. If we do not hinder its operation by voluntary distractions, and a kind of dissipation by which the devil seeks to make us lose all the fruit of Communion, it will work wonders in us.

(*Devotion to the Sacred Heart* - Father John Croiset, S.J.)

He begs for a little company. For hours and hours, He is all, all alone. Oh, what a longing – one that is well-nigh a necessity – He has for my presence! It would cost me so very little to give Him a few minutes every day; and still, rather than pay him a brief visit, I yawn and try to while away the weary hours. Rather than sit at His blessed feet, I would quite tire myself out in searching after the pleasures of the world and its miserable distractions!

Jesus begs for a little love.

Contemplate Him, O my soul...Not far from Him there stands another; also he would have something of you...it is Satan!

(*Eucharistic Whisperings* - Father Winfrid Herbst, S.D.S.)

...For sinners, the door of His heart is always open, so that He will never drive them away, however miserable they may be.

He so earnestly desired the salvation of sinners that He did not cease until He was nailed to a cross between two thieves and shed His Precious Blood for them. Not content with this, having finished the course of His earthly life, He instituted this Sacrament [the Eucharist] by which He might remain among men, so that all who need a remedy would always find it. The same cause that led Him to die for sinners, led Him to institute this Sacrament. It was love that brought Him down to earth and put Him in the hands of sinners; it is love also that brings Him back again and puts Him in the same hands. There was no other cause for this Great work but love on His part and need on our part. Therefore, this Sacrament is a common remedy for the just and for sinners.

This is what they do not understand who stay away from this Sacrament. They do not realize that this Sacrament was instituted not only as food for the healthy, but as medicine for the sick; not only as a gift for the just, but as a remedy for repentant sinners. And he who is weaker needs this Sacrament more. The weak man is much less able to live than the strong. The strong man can go for a longer time without help, but he who is so weak that as soon as God's eyes are turned from him he begins to fall away, where will he end if he does not use this aid?

Therefore, the Lord especially compassionated this type of person when He said: 'If I let them go away hungry, they will fall by the wayside, because some of them have come from afar.' Then as now those who have come from afar were in greater danger because they have had a longer journey; so also the weak suffer more because they have yet a long way to travel before they reach the perfection of charity. And since this heavenly bread was meant as a help for such as these, it is not temerity but a very salutary prudence to make use of this remedy and medicine which has been provided by Him at the cost of no less love than blood. One of the great faults of men and for which they shall one day have to give an accounting, is that they have not taken advantage of the remedy of the Blessed Sacrament.

(*Summa of a Christian Life – Preparation for Communion* - Venerable Louis of Granada, O.P.)

For centuries, I have carried in My Heart a sorrowful cross. How many souls are there redeemed by My Blood, yet, definitely lost! Although destined to be consumed in the fires of My Love, they have already fallen by thousands into the terrible and avenging flames. Yet they belonged to Me!

Listen to them. From the depths of hell, they curse the crib of Bethlehem, My poverty, and My appeals to the World. They curse the blood-stained Cross imprinted on their conscience. They curse My Church which offered them the treasures of Redemption. They curse My Eucharist, they who would have spent eternity in bliss if they had been nourished by the bread of immortality, which I offer them in the Blessed Sacrament.

Yet how many of these unfortunate souls like you came to kneel at My feet but afterwards, yielding to the world, chose for themselves their hell.

I called them constantly, I pursued them, I embraced them with the tenderness of a God, but one day they broke their chains, they pulled themselves violently away from My embrace, and in their mad frenzy, chose a sinful gratification at the price of endless woe!

At this very moment, they curse Me with a curse that will now be eternal! And, sorrow of sorrows, they were Mine! It was especially because of them, at the sight of their irrevocable loss, that My Heart was breaking in the Garden of Gethsemane, for they were all My children!

Look beloved souls! From the intensity of this unspeakable anguish, the Wound in My Heart is open and will remain open, yes, open, that you who love Me may find there superabundant life, a Heaven. Life eternal.

(*Twenty Holy Hours* - Rev. Mateo Crawley-Boevey, SS.CC.)

Wherever I may be, I will often think of Jesus in the Blessed Sacrament. I will fix my thoughts on the holy Tabernacle - even when I happen to wake up at night - adoring Him from where I am, calling to Jesus in the Blessed Sacrament, offering up to Him the action I am performing.

I will install one telegraph cable from my study to the church, another from my bedroom, and a third from our refectory; and as often as I can, I will send messages of love to Jesus in the Blessed Sacrament.

The occupation of a fervent soul at this time [at the reception of Holy Communion], should be principally, to abandon herself entirely to the love of her Divine Savior, and to enjoy the sweetness of His presence.

A tender and sincere love is, at the same time, the best disposition for Communion, and the chief fruit we should draw from it. A soul that loves much, is generally silent in the presence of Jesus Christ, and shows her love for Him, by fervent interior acts.

Magdalen lost in admiration at our Savior's feet, is the model of a soul that has communicated. If she speaks, her words must only be expressions of her love, her admiration, and her joy.

(*Devotion to the Sacred Heart* - Father John Croiset, S.J.)

...There is a very real sense in which the prayer of adoration is a loss of one's life. It is a kind of falling into the ground to die. Remember this when you come to adore Me.

Look at the Sacred Host and see Me who am the grain of wheat fallen into the ground and risen to life, and become the food of a vast multitude of souls, and this until the end of time. The grain of wheat that I was has become the Host that I am.

When you adore Me, forgetting yourself and forsaking all things for Me, you imitate Me, for adoration is a kind of death. It is a passing out of everything that solicits the senses and a cleaving to Me alone in the bright darkness of faith. So it will be in the hour of your death.

The more deeply you sink into adoration, the more deeply are you planted in the earth, there to die, and there to sprout, and finally to bring forth much fruit.

Sink into the ground of adoration. Consent to disappear, to forsake appearances, and to die. Enter into the silence of the Host. Become by grace what you contemplate in faith: Here I am hidden, silent, and forsaken by all save a very few whom I have chosen to enter into my hiddenness, my silence, and my solitude.

If you would serve Me, follow Me into my Eucharistic state. Lose all that the world counts as something and become with Me something that the world counts as nothing.

(In Senu Jesu – When Heart Speaks to Heart - The Journal of a Priest)

The Voice of Jesus: My children, offer Me your love and your fervent prayers. Give Me the holocaust of your generous sacrifices in order to conquer so many souls who struggle against the outpouring tenderness of My Heart which pleads without truce or rest.

Count, if you can, the bloody thorns of My Crown. Perhaps you will find there the well-beloved name of someone from your own family circle. How many consolations and thoughtful kindnesses I have offered to them only to have them rejected by these very ones so dear to your heart and Mine! Perhaps they are not wicked, but forgetful of Me they live carried away by the cares and pleasures of the world. Pray, faithful souls, pray that the patience and infinite mercy of My Heart triumph over their resistance, and that one day I may win a great victory here in My Eucharist, where My love awaits them.

I thirst with a burning thirst to see Myself surrounded in this Host by a happy and numerous army of returned prodigals, of recovered lost sheep, of sinners converted by the gentleness of My reproaches, by My tears, and by the choice graces promised and granted through the Holy Hour and through the fervent celebration of First Fridays. Why are you waiting? Ask, dear apostles, ask with faith, for the God of Love Who is here, has willed His captivity on the Altar only to give happiness to the world. Knock with perfect confidence, knock again on the Wound in My Side, and the doors of My Heart will open wide to you.

(Twenty Holy Hours - Rev. Mateo Crawley-Boevey, SS.CC)

There are times when physical lassitude, cold or heat, an importunate thought, a trial with its sting still fresh, baffles every effort to fix the mind on the subject of prayer, and concentrates the whole attention on what for the moment is all-absorbing.

Times harder still to manage, when mind and heart are so absolutely vacant and callous that there is no rousing them to action.

This reflection will sometimes be helpful then: What should I have to say were I in the presence of the one I loved best in the world; with whom I am quite at my ease; my friend *par excellence*; to whom my trials, difficulties, character, the secrets of my soul are known; that one in whose concerns and welfare I take the deepest interest; whose plans and views are mine, discussed again and again together; in whose company time flies and the hour of parting comes too soon – what should I find to say?

Say it, make an effort to say it to Him Who is in the tabernacle yonder.

(*Coram Sanctissimo* – Mother Mary Loyola)

Jesus: My friends, behold the Heart which has loved you beyond description, even far beyond the crucifixion of My body and soul on Calvary; see the Heart which has loved you to the complete giving of Itself, this Heart which will keep Me your prisoner forever, your captive in the Holy Tabernacle. Here in the divine Eucharist, I have exhausted My inexhaustible love. Sad to say, it is also here that man comes to exhaust his boundless ingratitude!

You parents, naturally so sensitive, whose hearts have suffered so much from cruel hurts inflicted by your own children whom you have often spoiled, add up, if you can, all your bitterness, add that to all the tears shed since the beginning of the world, in the garden of Paradise. All of that is but a drop of water compared to the fathomless, shoreless ocean of My anguish on the holy Altar.

Come close to Me, all of you who are bruised by deception and pierced to the heart by your own at home; come, you who are crushed by injustice, tortured by cruel separations by misfortunes and anguish often more sorrowful than death itself! You who are deprived of prosperity here below also come, all of you whose souls are torn in shreds! Finally, you who have tasted the chalice of all griefs, and have been touched by all the cruelties of life, come to Me, not only to be consoled, but that you may understand in the light of the Tabernacle as Christians, that the torrent of your misfortunes is only a drop of that flood that God the Father pours on His Son, your hidden God.

In this prison, I expiate the ingratitude of men who forget their God and wound their Savior as the most ungrateful of sons overwhelm their parents with shame and anguish!

See Me disdained, put in the last place, forgotten even as the most ordinary of friends would not be forgotten; despised even as the worst scoundrel would not be despised. And yet, I am the King, the Savior of the world. I am Jesus, your God and your brother. My friends, have pity on My soul, sorrowful unto death!

I do not return forgetfulness for forgetfulness. My revenge is love! That is why from the depths of My prison, I tearfully follow the multitude of children who never receive Holy Communion, though they have been redeemed by My blood!

They live by My side; our houses are close together; I have given them a home, bread for their table, and comforts that should remind them of Me. But they have never come to My door, asking for Me, the Bread of eternal life. And these children will die of hunger just outside their Father's house!

My children, what shall I say now of the many who have experienced the love of My Heart in the Holy Eucharist a thousand and one times, and then have forgotten Me and left Me, never to return! I always wait for them, but in vain. Their ingratitude transpierces My soul and rends it bitterly.

Finally, see the innumerable souls made giddy by the pleasures of the world, who more out of fear than love grudgingly devote to the God of the Tabernacle, an occasional few minutes snatched from their own concerns and from creatures. Moreover, they are convinced, that in approaching Me they pay Me quite a gratuitous honor. Even if the little they do were well done. But they quickly go away; they are in such a hurry it would seem as if they had not a moment for Him who reserves and offers them an eternity.

(*Twenty Holy Hours* - Rev. Mateo Crawley-Boevey, SS.CC.)

Faith allows you to see that your hands and lips that receive Jesus are always unclean - even when you are in a state of sanctifying grace - because you are always a sinner, and the hands and lips of a sinner always remain unworthy and, therefore, unclean...Just think, you receive Jesus with your lips that can kill with words. Your words sometimes wound and are the source of harm and unhappiness, instead of uttering blessings. And yet, these sinful lips come into contact with the highest sanctity of God. If you consider all of this, you will come to know the mystery that theology call *kenosis* (Greek: a complete humiliation).

The Eucharist is a *kenosis* - the Self-humiliation of true God and true Man, since Jesus in His utmost sanctity comes into contact with your sinfulness and your unworthiness. This does not mean, however, that you should avoid the Eucharist, for when you receive the Eucharist, He makes you more worthy of receiving Him again. Jesus waits for you with His love. He wants to come in order to transform you, to sanctify you, and to make you increasingly more worthy of His coming...

See Him in the tabernacle; fix your eyes on Him who is the light; bring your hearts close to His Divine Heart; ask Him to grant you the grace of knowing Him, the love of loving Him, the courage to serve Him. Seek Him fervently.

(Saint Teresa of Calcutta)

O Lover of men, so lonely, so forsaken, if Your object in staying with us day and night was to win our love, have You not failed?

Has it been worth Your while to work miracle after miracle to produce Your Real Presence upon the altar? Have I made it worth Your while to be there *for me*? Jesus, dear Jesus, I bury my face in my hands; I know of no heart more ungrateful, more callous than my own. I have been miserably unmindful of Your Presence here *for me*. I have let self, pleasure, troubles even – anything and everything furnish an excuse for keeping away from You and neglecting You in that Sacramental life which is lived here *for me*.

(*Coram Sanctissimo* - Mother Mary Loyola)

Hence, if my Communion is truly holy and worthy, if Jesus does not find in me the obstacle of sin, He, in a certain sense, deifies me and all my works...then everything – even things that would otherwise have no value whatsoever – become of infinite and supernatural value within me, thanks to Holy

Communion. So, for instance, my recreations, my work become the recreations and the work of Jesus; the breath I take at rest and in toil becomes the breath of Jesus. When I come and go, Jesus comes and goes; when I sit at table, Jesus sits at table. In short, no matter what I do it is Jesus who does it.

Oh, what a consoling thought this is! I can lead a humble life, a life hidden from the eyes of men, unknown, apparently useless, even despised; and at the same time, I may rest assured that it is the opposite in the eyes of the omnipotent God, that it is holy and, therefore, most useful and abounding in the blessings for the whole human race – for Jesus lives in me! What greatness! What honor! What a consolation for the poor and despised!...The trouble is that I do not sufficiently realize this, I do not think of it. But is nevertheless true…

(*Eucharistic Whisperings* - Father Winfrid Herbst, S.D.S.)

We must endeavor at that time [at the reception of Holy Communion], to enter into the sentiments of Jesus Christ, and consider what displeases Him in us, what are His designs upon us, what He wills we should do, and what can hinder us in the future from doing what He desires.

Let us remain in spirit at His feet, and renewing from time to time, our faith in the presence of Jesus Christ, let us adore Him with profound respect, mingled with fear, seeing that this God of Majesty, before Whom the Seraphim tremble, humbles Himself as far as to dwelling in the heart of a mortal man and a sinner...He destroys the laws of nature, and works such stupendous miracles. Then passing from sentiments of admiration to those of gratitude, let us, with a sense of our absolute incapability of testifying it sufficiently to our Lord, invite all creatures to bless Him with us.

Let us offer to Him the love which all the Blessed feel for Him, and the fervor with which so many holy souls communicate.

Let us offer Him His Own Heart, with the immense love that inflames it.

Let us then unfold to Him, with great confidence and sincerity, our weaknesses, our miseries, and our wants.

(*Devotion to the Sacred Heart* - Father John Croiset, S.J.)

Presently, my children, when I shall hold Our Lord in my hands, when the good God blesses you, ask Him to open the eyes of your heart; say to Him with the blind man of Jericho, '0 Lord, make me to see!' If you say to Him sincerely, 'Make me to see,' you will certainly obtain what you desire, because He wishes nothing but your happiness. He has His hands full of graces seeking someone to whom to distribute them, but alas, no one will have them...! Oh, indifference! Oh, ingratitude! My children, we are most unhappy not to understand these things! We shall understand them well one day, but it will then be too late.

(*The Holy Eucharist Our All* - Father Lukas Etlin, O.S.B quoting Saint John Vianney)

...I filled Your soul in the Garden of Gethsemani with fear and sorrow even unto death; now I will comfort it and make it rejoice by fervent Holy Communion and loving visits to You in this Sacrament of Your love. I bound Your Body to a pillar and scourged it so unmercifully that Your Sacred Flesh was torn to fragments and Your Precious Blood flowed in streams to the ground; now I will receive that Divine Body devoutly and often, and each time I will solemnly promise never again to let my passions hurt You in any way. ...Yes, I condemned You to death. 0 dear Jesus, now I am going to visit You often in Your earthly dwelling place; here I am going to offer my life to You; here, with You and from You, I am going to seek the life of grace and the pledge of life everlasting...

(Eucharistic Whisperings - Father Winfrid Herbst, S.D.S.)

Encountering Christ in adoration of the Blessed Sacrament is an invitation, for all people, to deepen their relationship with the Lord, and to grow in communion with His Church. In adoration, we grow in unity and friendship with Him—we learn to hear His voice, to know His will, and, most especially, to know and trust the power of His love.

Everyone - no matter his circumstances - can kneel before the Eucharist, and encounter, in visible reality, the mystery of God's transformative and powerful love. We all long for love, and in the gift of Eucharistic adoration, we can all experience the love of the Lord.

No one needs to be a mystic to kneel before the Lord in adoration. Everyone begins the practice of prayer without knowing much about how to pray. But in silence, kneeling before Jesus, we learn how God speaks to us. We learn to hear his 'still, small voice,' and we learn to speak to God from the depths of our own hearts. In silence, we learn to put aside the plaguing distractions of our time - the chirping and buzzing of our technology - and simply experience the presence of God, which transforms us in peace.

'God's first language,' said Saint John of the Cross, 'is silence.' In the silence of Eucharistic adoration, we learn true humility. As we kneel before our Creator-God, we are confronted with the power and the mystery of God's love.

And it is from this silence and humility that we experience a deep communion and friendship with God.

(A Pastoral Letter on Adoration of the Most Holy Eucharist - Bishop James Conley)

What shall I answer if I have not responded to the love of Jesus – and not given Him the whole love of my heart – and not spent myself for Him Who loved me unto death, even unto the death of the Cross? What shall I answer when I find out that throughout my life, every hour of the day and night, Jesus was for me imprisoned in the tabernacle, pleading for me with the Father – wishing for me to visit Him, to unite Himself to me, and to be my faithful, my own God?

(Meditation on the Passion - A Mistress of Novices of the Institute of the Blessed Virgin Mary)

If we knew we could find Him anywhere on earth, we would try to go there. We have Him, every free moment, on the altar. Be with Him there.

(Venerable Edel Mary Quinn)

We ministers of the Lord, for whom the Tabernacle has become mute and silent, the stone of consecration cold, the Host a venerable, but lifeless, memento: have been unable to turn souls from their evil. How could we ever draw them out of the mire or forbidden pleasures?

(The Soul of the Apostolate - Jean-Baptiste Chautard, O.C.S.O.)

O what an awesome thought! You deal otherwise with others, but, as to me, the flesh and blood of God is my sole life. I shall perish without it; yet shall I not perish with it and by it? How can I raise myself to such an act as to feed upon God? 0 my God, I am in a quandary - shall I go forward, or shall I go back?

I will go forward: I will go to meet You. I will open my mouth, and receive Your gift. I do so with great awe and fear, but what else can I do? To whom should I go but to You? Who can save me but You? Who can cleanse me but You? Who can make me overcome myself but You? Who can raise my body from the grave but You? Therefore, I come to You in all these my necessities: in fear, but in faith.

(*For You My Soul Has Thirsted* - Blessed John Henry Cardinal Newman)

Jesus wants me to tell you again…how much love He has for each one of you – beyond all you can imagine. I worry some of you still have not really met Jesus – one to one – you and Jesus alone. We may spend time in chapel – but have you seen with the eyes of your soul how He looks at you with love? Do you really know the living Jesus – not from books but from being with Him in your heart? Have you heard the loving words He speaks to you? Ask for the grace, He is longing to give it. Until you hear Jesus in the silence of your own heart, you will not be able to hear Him saying 'I Thirst' in the hearts of the poor.

(From Mother Teresa's Letter to the Missionaries of Charity Family – March 25, 1993)

Final Exhortation

The greatest tragedy in our world today is the failure to believe that our Lord and Savior Jesus Christ is really, truly and substantially present in the Blessed Sacrament – a Prisoner of love - hidden in the tabernacles of locked church buildings, where for the most part He is abandoned, ignored and unappreciated!

The sad but truthful reality is that in far too many of our churches we have lost the sense of the Sacred and an appreciation for the Holy Sacrifice of the Mass that are essential for fostering and maintaining a belief in the Real Presence.

We need Bishops, priests religious and laypeople to get on their knees before their Eucharistic Lord. It is He, not any of them, Who will gift us with a deep, abiding, life-changing, sanctifying belief in His Real Human and Divine Presence here among us. Everything else we need or think we need individually or as Church will flow from Him.

So what can we simple people do about all of this? Listen to the prophets among us. Among those voices resonating in the Church today is Father Mark Daniel Kirby, O.S.B. whose love for our Eucharistic Lord and his brother priests know no bounds. His blog, *Vultus Christi*, and recently published book, *In Senu Jesu: When Heart Speaks to Heart – The Journal of a Priest at Prayer*, are must reads for anyone who loves God and wants to take His call to personal holiness seriously.

With the good Father's indulgence, I am setting forth one of the more poignant excerpts from *In Senu Jesu*, one that I am asking everyone reading this book to copy and give to their

Bishops and priests – every Bishop and every priest in this country.

Impractical and impossible goal, you say? You are right unless God wills it!

The simple man writing this is convinced there is nothing of more value that any of us can do today than to pass the following reflection on as requested. Tell everyone you know on Facebook, Twitter, Google and other social media of this request.

Let's see God do the impossible because one humble priest has the courage to speak the truth and we simple people responded. God is counting on you!

We can do it!

Love's Invisible Radiance

There are so many tabernacles on earth where I am, for all intents and purposes, like one buried, hidden, forgotten, and out of sight. My Divine radiance is diminished because there are so few adorers to act as the receptors of My radiant Eucharistic love and to extend My radiance through space and into the universe of souls.

Where there is faith in My Real Presence, there will be adoration; and where there is adoration, there will also be an efficacious radiance of My presence drawing souls to My Eucharistic Heart and surrounding them, even at a distance, with the healing influence of My Eucharistic Face.

In those places where I am exposed upon the altar to receive the adoration, the reparation, and the companionship of My friends - and, first of all, of My priests - My radiance is powerful and strong.

Faith, adoration, and love act as receptors; thus is My power drawn out and made effective, invisibly but really, in space and in time.

It was the same with My Sacred Humanity during My life on earth; the faith and love of My friends drew out the virtue of My Divinity, and an invisible radiance acted in souls, and upon them, bringing healing, holiness, and many graces of conversion. When I am adored in a place, My hidden action upon souls is wonderfully increased.

The place where I am adored becomes a radiant center from which love, and life, and light are diffused in a world in the grip of hatred, and darkness, and death. Chapels of adoration are not mere refuges for the devout. They are the radiant, pulsating centers of an intense divine activity that goes beyond the walls of the place where I am adored to penetrate homes, and schools, and hospitals; to reach even those dark and cold places wherein souls are enslaved to Satan; to penetrate hearts, heal the infirm, and call home those who have wandered far from Me. For these reasons, the work of perpetual adoration, or even of prolonged daily adoration, is intensely apostolic and supernaturally efficacious.

Would that My bishops understood this!

But, alas, they put their trust in human schemes, in plans devised by the worldly-wise, and in programs drawn-up along shortsighted human principles. And so they go, and they will continue to go from failure to failure, and from disillusionment to disillusionment.

I have not set bishops over My flock to govern, and to teach, and to sanctify, out of their personal abilities and by making use of the wisdom of this passing world. I have set them as lights upon a lampstand to shine in every dark place, and I have equipped them with supernatural gifts and divine power to accomplish that for which I chose them and set them over My Church.

Woe to those bishops who trust in purely human solutions to the problems that beset My Church. They will be grievously disappointed, and many souls will fall away because they have neglected to take up the supernatural weapons I have prepared for them in this time of spiritual combat.

My presence in the Blessed Sacrament preached, and confessed, and surrounded by adoration, love, and heartfelt reparation is the single greatest remedy for the evils that afflict My Church and for the sorrows that weigh so heavily upon My priests.

My ways are not your ways, nor do I act according to the principles of worldly success. I act in the silent, humble, hidden reality of My Eucharistic presence. Adore Me, and the radiance of My Eucharistic Face will begin to change the face of the earth, even as it heals My priests, calls sinners home to My Heart, and enlivens the hearts of those grown weary and sad (like the disciples on the road to Emmaus) with a spark of divine vitality and with the fire of My Eucharistic love.

I speak to you in this way not only for you, beloved friend of My Heart, but also for those who will receive these words, ponder them, and out of them draw the inspiration to love Me more generously, more fruitfully, and more joyfully.

I speak to you for the sake of My priests. You will be astonished at the reception given to these words of Mine. Many souls of priests will be quickened and consoled by them. Many priests will be moved to spend time in the radiance of My Eucharistic Face, and to abide close to My pierced Heart.

This is My desire for them. I want to draw all My priests into the radiance of My Face and, then, into the sanctuary of My open Heart.

(*In Sinu Iesu, When Heart Speaks to Heart - The Journal of a Priest*)

Ten Questions For Further Reflection

What if, as Father Francis Hudson, S.C.J. once asked his parishioners, God loved you, **only** as much as you loved Him?

Do you believe that Jesus is really, truly and substantially present in every Catholic Church and in the Sacred Host placed on your tongue?

As you enter your parish Church are you struck with a sense of the Sacred and a realization that you are standing on holy ground? If not, why not?

What does Jesus see and hear from behind the locked Tabernacle doors when He gazes at those present? Is He pleased by what He hears and sees? If not, why not?

How important is it for you to spend some time in quiet prayer and reflection in the presence of the Blessed Sacrament, before, during, after Mass and throughout the course of each week?

Are you satisfied with the manner in which you act and treat our Lord? If not, what changes do you intend to make?

What concrete things can you do to encourage yourself and others in your family and parish toward a greater reverence and belief in the God who dwells among us?

Which quotation or quotations in this book touched your heart and stirred your soul? Why?

Of the 168 hours God gives you each week, how much of that time do you even think of, talk to, or visit Him?

How much do you love God.?

Appendix A

Prayer of Reparation to the Eucharistic Heart of Jesus

O Lord Jesus Christ present in this wonderful Sacrament, I desire at this hour to make reparation to Thy Eucharistic Heart and to open myself to Thy Love for the sake of those who refuse or ignore it.

Increase Thou my faith, that I may believe firmly in the truths and mysteries Thou hast revealed to Thy Church, for the sake of those who do not believe.

By my attention to Thy Eucharistic Heart, I desire to make up for indifference to Thy Love, for coldness, and for irreverence in Thy Sacramental Presence. By my gratitude to Thy Eucharistic Heart, I desire to make up for ingratitude toward Thee Who remainest hidden and forgotten in the tabernacles of so many locked churches.

By my trust in Thy Eucharistic Heart, I desire to make up for those who do not trust Thee, for those who are afraid to trust Thee, and for those whose trust in Thy Love has been weakened by sins of scandal, by the weight of life's hardships, or by painful loss.

By my hope in Thy Eucharistic Heart, I desire to help those tempted to despair of Thy Mercy. Allow me, I beseech Thee, to hope for those who have no hope and, because Thou didst pour out Thy Blood for them, let not one of them be lost.

In spite of my weakness and inconstancy, I desire, by this humble act of reparation to obtain for all who yearn for Thy friendship, a share in the unspeakable sweetness experienced by Thy beloved disciple Saint John when he rested his head upon Thy Heart on the night before Thy Sacred Side was opened by the soldier's lance.

Let my desire to be open to the Love of Thy Eucharistic Heart serve to repair the brokenness of the most wounded and fragile members of Thy Mystical Body. By the mysterious workings of Thy Holy Spirit and the intercession of the Blessed Virgin Mary, let the reparation and adoration Thou hast inspired me to offer in Thy presence bring reconciliation to those alienated from Thy Church, healing to souls in need of Thy mercy, and choice graces to Thy priests. Amen.

(From *Vultus Christi*. Used with permission)

Appendix B

Testimonies of Adorers

I feel a warmth that surrounds my heart, so much love. I don't have this feeling anywhere else. I know Jesus is in me always, but to be in His Real Presence, in our Chapel, is the best hour of my day. I truly love coming, never mind subbing and never feel that it is an inconvenience. After all the years of coming, I still feel excited when I know I am going to do Adoration. I have been at Adoration during all hours of the day and night and I believe Adoration is one of the greatest gifts given to me by our Lord. You will not regret the time being here with Jesus. You will fall in love too!

****

Adoration has given me that moment each week to better focus my life, to be close, one-on-one with Jesus. To feel love and return it to my friends and family. To have the ability to ask and pray to Jesus for others in need along with myself. Adoration has opened my heart and has allowed me to see more clearly the miracle of 'The Mass' and Jesus is so much alive in all of us!

****

Since I started coming to Adoration most of the changes in my life have been internal. I have become a much more spiritual person as a result of the peace that I absorb during the short hour that I am in Christ's Presence. I am much better prepared when a crisis arises to deal with the problem with the knowledge that I am not in it alone. I have also become much more confident about speaking to others about my love for the Catholic Church and how following Jesus's teachings in the Gospels have not made me feel that I am confined to a set of rules but have made me feel free and loved unconditionally. Basically, coming to Adoration has enriched my life in countless ways. It has touched every aspect of my life from how I treat others, to how I spend my free time at home. Coming to Adoration will change your life! As Jesus said to His disciples: 'Could you not keep watch for one hour?' Come and see what the Lord will do for you.

****

Adoration has helped me in many ways. I started coming to adoration with my Mom when I was eight. I didn't come every week. I would just come once in a while. When I started having problems in school with my teacher and classmates, I came to Adoration and prayed to God or I wrote down my thoughts and thanked Him for helping me do better. God is always by your side wherever you go and helps you along the way. So, I encourage you to come to Adoration once a week to pray to God for one hour. I guarantee that if you sign up, something in your life will get better each time you come. So, come, sign up for Adoration and help your parish out. I did and God has helped me through many of my hardships.

****

Adoration is a resting place for my tired, hurried body and mind. Our dear God is my therapist, Who gives me peace. It is almost like I am transformed into a better person but then I'm turned out into the world and by the next week, I am ready for adoration and to be renewed. Adoration has made a positive difference in my life. I am thankful for God's goodness and I have seen miracles take place around me.

Appendix C

A PRAYER OF SAINT PADRE PIO AFTER COMMUNION

Stay with me, Lord, for it is necessary to have You present so that I do not forget You. You know how easily I abandon You.

Stay with me Lord, because I am weak, and I need Your strength, so that I may not fall so often.

Stay with me Lord, for You are my life, and without You, I am without fervor.

Stay with me Lord, for You are my light, and without you, I am in darkness.

Stay with me Lord, to show me Your will.

Stay with me Lord, so that I hear Your voice and follow You.

Stay with me Lord, for I desire to love you very much, and always be in Your Company.

Stay with me Lord, if You wish me to be faithful to You.

Stay with me Lord, for as poor as my soul is, I want it to be a place of consolation for You, a nest of Love.

Stay with me, Jesus, for it is getting late, and the day is coming to a close, and life passes, death, judgment, eternity approach. It is necessary to renew my strength, so that I will not stop along the way and for that, I need You. It is getting late and death approaches. I fear the darkness, the temptations, the dryness, the cross, the sorrows. O how I need You, my Jesus, in this night of exile.

Stay with me tonight, Jesus, in life with all its dangers, I need You.

Let me recognize You as Your disciples did at the breaking of bread, so that the Eucharistic Communion be the light which disperses the darkness, the force which sustains me, the unique joy of my heart.

Stay with me Lord, because at the hour of my death, I want to remain united to you, if not by Communion, at least by grace and love.

Stay with me Jesus, I do not ask for divine consolation because I do not merit it, but the gift of Your presence, oh yes, I ask this of You.

Stay with me Lord, for it is You alone I look for, Your Love, Your Grace, Your Will, Your Heart, Your Spirit, because I love You and ask no other reward but to love You more and more.

With a firm love, I will love You with all my heart while on earth and continue to love You perfectly during all eternity. Amen.

Appendix D

Prayer of Saint Maria Faustina Kowalska

O Blessed Host, in whom is contained the testament of God's mercy for us, and especially for poor sinners.

O Blessed Host, in whom is contained the Body and Blood of the Lord Jesus as proof of infinite mercy for us, and especially to poor sinners.

O Blessed Host, in whom is contained life eternal and of infinite mercy, dispensed in abundance to us and especially to poor sinners.

O Blessed Host, in whom is contained the mercy of the Father, the Son and the Holy Spirit toward us, and O Blessed Host especially toward poor sinners.

O Blessed Host, in whom is contained the infinite price of mercy which will compensate for all our debts, and especially those of poor sinners.

O Blessed Host, in whom is contained the fountain of living water which springs from infinite mercy for us, and especially for poor sinners.

O Blessed Host, in whom is contained the fire of purest love which blazes forth from the bosom of the Eternal Father, as from an abyss of infinite mercy for us, and especially for poor sinners.

O Blessed Host, in whom is contained the medicine for all our infirmities, flowing from infinite mercy, as from a fount, for us and especially for poor sinners.

O Blessed Host, in whom is contained the union between God and us through His infinite mercy for us, and especially for poor sinners.

O Blessed Host, in whom are contained all the sentiments of the most sweet Heart of Jesus toward us, and especially poor sinners.

O Blessed Host, our only hope in all the sufferings and adversities of life.

O Blessed Host, our only hope in the midst of darkness and of storms within and without.

O Blessed Host, our only hope in life and at the hour of our death.

O Blessed Host, our only hope in the midst of adversities and floods of despair.

O Blessed Host, our only hope in the midst of falsehood and treason.

O Blessed Host, our only hope in the midst of the darkness and godlessness which inundate the earth.

O Blessed Host, our only hope in the longing and pain in which no one will understand us.

O Blessed Host, our only hope in the toil and monotony of everyday life.

O Blessed Host, our only hope amid the ruin of our hopes and endeavors.

O Blessed Host, our only hope in the midst of the ravages of the enemy and the efforts of hell.

O Blessed Host, I trust in You when the burdens are beyond my strength and I find my efforts are fruitless.

O Blessed Host, I trust in You when storms toss my heart about and my fearful spirit tends to despair.

O Blessed Host, I trust in You when my heart is about to tremble and mortal sweat moistens my brow.

O Blessed Host, I trust in You when everything conspires against me and black despair creeps into my soul.

O Blessed Host, I trust in You when my eyes will begin to grow dim to all temporal things and, for the first time, my spirit will behold the unknown worlds.

O Blessed Host, I trust in You when my tasks will be beyond my strength and adversity will become my daily lot.

O Blessed Host, I trust in You when the practice of virtue will appear difficult for me and my nature will grow rebellious.

O Blessed Host, I trust in You when hostile blows will be aimed against me.

O Blessed Host, I trust in You when my toils and efforts will be misjudged by others.

O Blessed Host, I trust in You when Your judgments will resound over me; it is then that I will trust in the Sea of Your Mercy.

(Prayer of Saint Faustina while in Adoration of the Blessed Sacrament from *The Diary of Saint Maria Faustina Kowalska: Divine Mercy in My Soul* (356) Used with permission

Permissions Granted

Reasonable care has been taken to trace ownership and, when necessary, to obtain permission for quotations included in this book. The author gratefully acknowledges permissions granted to reprint excerpts from the following sources:

Angelico Press from *In Senu Jesu – When Heart Speaks to Heart – The Journal of a Priest at Prayer*, Kettering, OH. © 2016

Catholic Way Publishing from *The Catholic Collection: 734 Catholic Essays and Novels on Authentic Catholic Teaching*, © 2013

Baronius Press, www.baroniuspress.com
from *Divine Intimacy - Meditations on the Interior Life for Every Day of the Liturgical Year*, by Father Gabriel of St. Mary Magdalen, © Monastero S. Giuseppe – Carmelitane Scalze

Ignatius Press (http://www.ignatius.com) from *Could You Not Watch with Me One Hour? - How to Cultivate a Deeper Relationship with the Lord through Eucharistic Adoration* by- Father Florian Racine, San Francisco, CA. ©2014. Used with permission.

Marian Press from *The Dairy of St. Maria Faustina Kowalska: Divine Mercy in My Soul*, Marian Fathers of the Immaculate Conception, Stockbridge, MA 01263 © 1987. Used with permission.

National Sacred Heart Enthronement Center from *Twenty Holy Hours* by Rev. Mateo Crawley-Boevey, SS.CC., National Sacred Heart Enthronement Center, Fairhaven, MA. © 1992

Silverstream Monastery, Benedictine Monks of Perpetual Adoration, excerpts from their blog, *Vultus Christi*, entitled *Thursday of Adoration and Reparation for Priests* and *Prayer of Reparation to the Eucharistic Heart of Jesus*, Stamullen County Mead Ireland © 2013-2017

Alphabetical Index of Individuals Quoted

A

Thomas a Kempis (1379 -1471) priest, monk and writer

James L. Alberione (Blessed) (1884 -1971) Founder of Society of St. Paul and the Daughters of St. Paul

Albert the Great, O.P. (Saint) (340-397) Dominican priest, scientist, philosopher, theologian, Bishop, and Doctor of the Church

Thomas Aquinas, O.P. (Saint) (1225-1274) Italian Dominican priest, philosopher, theologian, Doctor of the Church

B

John Baptiste de la Salle (Saint) (1651-1719) French priest, Patron of Christian educators and founder of the Institute of the Brothers of Christian Schools

Dina Belanger (Blessed) (1897-1929) Canadian religious, musician, and mystic

Benedict XVI (Pope) German priest, professor, theologian, author, Cardinal and Pope

Andre Bessette (Saint) (1845-1937) great devotion to St. Joseph, known as the "Miracle man of Montreal"; served as doorkeeper for many years at Notre Dame College; his efforts led to the building of St. Joseph's Oratory

Giovanni Bona (Cardinal) (1609-1674) Italian cardinal, author and Cistercian

M. Eugene Boylan, O.C.R. (Father) (1904-1963) Irish born Trappist monk and writer

Eustace Boylan, S.J. (Father) (1869-1953) entered Jesuits in Ireland and sent to Australia where he taught and wrote

Bridget (Saint) (1303-1373) Visions of Christ crucified from childhood, married to Swedish King Magnus II, mother of eight children, and co-patroness of Europe

Pere Jacques de Jesus Bunel, O.C.D. (Servant of God) (1900-1945) Carmelite friar, headmaster and Nazi concentration camp survivor

C

Raniero Cantalamessa, O.F.M. Cap, (Father) (1934 -) Italian Franciscan priest and theologian who has served as the Preacher to the Papal Household for John Paul II, Benedict XVI and Pope Francis

John J. Carberry (Cardinal) (1994-1998) Canon lawyer, pro-life advocate who led the Archdiocese of St Louis for 11 years

Concepcion Carbrera de Armida (1862-1937) Mexican widow, mystic and spiritual writer

Catherine of Siena (Saint) (1347-1380) Lay tertiary of the Dominican Order, mystic, Doctor of the Church, one of the two patron saints of Italy

J.B. Marcellin Champagnat (Saint) (1789-1840) French priest who founded the Marist Brothers

Jean Baptiste Chautard, O.C.S.O. (1858-1935) French Trappist abbot and spiritual writer

Charles de Foucald (Brother Charles of Jesus) (1858-1916) former French army officer, lived an eremitical life as a priest in the Sahara of Algeria, and martyr

John Chrysostom (Saint) (344-407) Eloquent preacher, theologian, liturgist, Archbishop of Constantinople, and a Doctor of the Church

Anthony Marie Claret (Saint) (1807-1870) Founder of the Missionary Sons of the Immaculate Heart of Mary (Claretians), Archbishop of Santiago, Cuba, and confessor to Queen Isabella II of Spain.

Mother Louise Margaret Claret, (Venerable) (1868-1915) French religious and founder of religious community whose purpose was to offer prayer and self-sacrifice for the Church and its priests

Claude de la Colombiere (Saint) (1641-1682) Jesuit priest, confessor to St. Margaret Mary Alacoque, and zealous apostle of the devotion to the Sacred Heart of Jesus

James Conley (Bishop) (1955 -) current Bishop of the Diocese of Lincoln Nebraska

Mateo Crawley-Boevey, SS.CC. (Father) (1875-1960) his life centered around the Eucharist, zeal for the salvation of souls and promotion of family enthronement to the Sacred Heart

Cristina de Artega (Sister) (1902-1984) Spanish nun, prioress, writer, poet and historian

John, Croiset, S.J. (Father) (1647-1690) French Jesuit priest, author, spiritual adviser to St. Margaret Mary Alacoque, and promoter of Devotion to the Sacred Heart

D

Damian of Molokai (Father) (Saint) (1840-1889) Belgium priest, member of the Congregation of the Sacred Hearts of Jesus and Mary and missionary to the lepers on the island of Molokai in Hawaii

Dorothy Day (Servant of God) (1897-1980) Journalist, social activist, Catholic convert, and with Peter Maurin, co-founder of the Catholic Worker Movement

Catherine Doherty (1896-1945) Wife, mother, social activist, author and founder of the Madonna House Apostolate, a Catholic community of lay men, women, and priests

E

Lukas Etlin, O.S.B. (Father) (1864-1927) Swiss born Benedictine and artist who moved to Missouri and lived with the Benedictines in Conception Abbey. The Eucharist was his great love.

Jose Marie Escriva (Saint) (1902-1975) Spanish priest, author, and founder of *Opus Dei*

John Eudes (Saint) (1601-1680) French missionary priest, founder of two religious orders (Congregation of Jesus and Mary and the Sisters of Our Lady of Charity)

Eugene de Mazenod (Saint) (1782-1861) French priest and Bishop who had a great passion for the poor, youth and prisoners

Peter Julian Eymard (Saint) (1811-1868) French Catholic priest, an Apostle of the Eucharist, and founder of two religious orders, the Congregation of the Blessed Sacrament and the Servants of the Blessed Sacrament

F

Frederick William Faber (Father) (1814-1863) Noted Anglican convert who became a Catholic priest, theologian and hymn writer

Marie Faustina Kowalska (Saint) (1905-1938) member of the Congregation of the Sisters of Our Lady of Mercy, spiritual writer, known as Apostle of Divine Mercy

Richard Foley, S.J. (Father) (+2003) English Jesuit known for his books, sermons and frequent appearances on EWTN.

Francis de Sales (Saint) 1567-1622) Bishop of Geneva, preacher and spiritual writer

Pier Giorgio Frassati (Blessed) (1901-1925) An Italian Lay Dominican who spent his young life in works of charity, prayer and social action.

G

Gabriel of St. Mary Magdalen, O.C.D. (Father) (1893-1953) Carmelite priest, author and spiritual director

Gemma Galgani (Saint) (1878-1903) Italian lay woman, stigmatist and mystic

John Hardon, S.J. (Father) (1914-2000) Jesuit priest, theologian, author, and founder of Holy Trinity Apostolate

Marie Estelle Harpain (1814-1842) writer and lover of the Eucharist

Winfrid Herbst, S.D.S. (Father.) (1891-1988) Salvatorian priest and spiritual writer

Caryll Houselander (1901-1954) Catholic artist, mystic, religious writer and poet

J

John XXIII (Saint) (Pope) (1881-1963) Reigned as Pope from 1958-1963 and convened Vatican Council II

John Paul II (Saint) (1920-2005) Pope from 1978-2005, second longest pontificate

Jeanne Jugan (Saint) (1792-1879) a French shepherdess who went on to found the Little Sisters of the poor to care for the elderly poor.

K

Louis Kaczmarek (+2015) author and official escort of the original Pilgrim Virgin Statute from Fatima

Raphael Kalinowski, O.C.D. (Saint) (1835-1907) Polish Discalced Carmelite friar, teacher and prisoner of war

John A. Kane, (Father) (1883-1962) Priest, author and first pastor in the Archdiocese of Philadelphia to introduce all-night Adoration of the Blessed Sacrament

Louis Kebreau, S.D.B. (1938 -   ) Archbishop Emeritus of Cap Haltien

Maximilian Kolbe (Saint) (1894-1941) Polish Conventual Franciscan friar, martyr, and known as the Apostle of Consecration to Mary

Peter Kreeft, Ph.D., Professor of Philosophy at Boston College, conference speaker, and prolific contemporary author

John Kronstadt (Saint) (1829-1908) Russian Orthodox priest

L

Catherine Laboure (Saint) 1806-1876) French member of the Daughters of Charity who relayed the Blessed Mother's request for the Miraculous Medal

Alphonsus Liguori (Saint) (1698-1787) Italian Bishop, spiritual writer, theologian, and founder of the Redemptorists

Louis of Granada, O.P. (Venerable) (1505-1588) Dominican theologian, preacher and writer

Lawrence G Lovasik, S.V.D. (Father) (1913-1986) Missionary in America's coal and steel regions, spiritual writer and founder of the Sisters of the Divine Spirit

Mother Mary Loyola (1845-1930) British religious sister and author of devotional books who lived in the Bar Convent in York, England

M

Margaret Mary Alacoque (Saint) (1647-1690) Member of the Visitation Order, known as Apostle to the Devotion of the Sacred Heart of Jesus

Mary of Agreda (Blessed) (1602-1665) Spanish Franciscan abbess and spiritual writer

Columba Marmon, O.S.B. (Blessed) (1858-1923) Irish Benedictine monk, Abbot and extraordinary spiritual writer

Josefa Menendez (Sister) (1890-1923) Spanish mystic who joined the Order of the Sacred Heart of Jesus in France

Thomas More (Saint) (1478-1535) English lawyer, philosopher, statesman and counsel to King Henry VIII, killed for defending the Catholic Faith, and patron saint of lawyers

Anselm Moynihan, O.P. (Father) contemporary Irish Dominican priest and author

Michael Muller, C.S.S.R. (Father) (1825-1899) Redemptorist priest and spiritual director

N

John Henry Cardinal Newman (Blessed) (1801-1890) Anglican convert to Catholicism, author and Cardinal

P

Anthony J. Paone, S.J. (Father) Jesuit priest who authored *My Daily Bread* in 1954

Mauro Piacenza (Cardinal) (1944 -) former Prefect of the Congregation for the Clergy

Peter Anastasius Pichenot, Bishop Diocese of Tarbes in which Lourdes is located; served from 1870-1873

Pio of Pietrelcina (Saint) (1887-1968) Capuchin priest, confessor, healer, mystic, and stigmatist

Pius VII (Servant of God) (Pope) (1742-1823) excommunicated Napoleon and later taken to France as a prisoner

Pius XI (Pope) (1857-1939) Served from February 6, 1922 to February 10, 1939

Pius XII (Venerable) (Pope) (1876-1958) Pope from March 2, 1939 to October 9, 1958

Q

Edel Mary Quinn (Venerable) (1907-1944) Lay Irish missionary whose poor health precluded her from entering a religious order

R

Florian Racine (Father) French priest and spiritual writer. Organized Missionaries of the Most Holy Eucharist to promote perpetual Eucharistic Adoration in parishes

M. Raymond, O.C.S.O. (Father) (1903-1990) Trappist priest and spiritual writer, born in 1903

Fulton J. Sheen (Venerable) (1895-1979) Archbishop, renowned theologian, prolific writer and television and radio evangelist

Bernadette Soubirous (Saint) (1844-1879) The Blessed Mother appeared to Bernadette at Lourdes, France identifying herself as the Immaculate Conception

Frederick Suarez (Father) (1917-) Spanish priest, author, professor and member of *Opus Dei*
T

Teresa Benedicta of the Cross (Edith Stein) (Saint) (1891-1942) German-Jewish philosopher, convert to Catholicism, Carmelite nun, martyred at Auschwitz

Teresa of the Andes (Saint) (1900-1920) a Chilean Discalced Carmelite, also known as Teresa of Jesus

Teresa of Avila (Saint) (1515-1582) Reformer of the Carmelite Order, Doctor of the Church and spiritual writer

Teresa of Calcutta (Saint) (1910-1997) Founder of the Missionary Sisters of Charity. Nobel Peace Prize winner.

Jose Guadalupe Trevino (Father) (1889 - +) Mexican priest, spiritual writer, and member of the Congregation of Missionaries of the Holy Ghost

V

John Marie Vianney (Saint) (1786-1859) Patron saint of all priests, known Cure of Ars

<u>Suggested Reading</u>

Thomas a Kempis. *The Imitation of Christ*. New York: Catholic Publishing Co., 1993, 1988, 1977

Margaret Mary Alacoque. *The Autobiography of Saint Margaret Mary*. Rockford, IL: TAN Books and Publishers.*1986*

Benedictine Priest. *In Sinu Iesu-When Heart Speaks to Heart -The Journal of a Priest*. Kettering, OH. Angelico Press. 2016

Eustace Boylan, S.J. *The Real Presence*. *https://www.ecatholic2000.com/cts/untitled-610.shtml*

Catholic Way Publishing. T*he Catholic Collection: 734 Catholic Essays and Novels on Authentic Catholic Teaching*, © 2013

Mateo Crawley-Boevery, SS.CC. *20 Holy Hours*. Boston, MA. Pauline Books and Media. 1992

Concepcion Cabrera de Armida - *Holy Hours*. Published by ST Pauls (www.stpauls.us)

John Cardinal Carberry. *Reflections and Prayers for Visits with our Eucharistic Lord*. Boston, MA: Pauline Books and Media. 1977

Catherine of Siena. *The Dialogue of St. Catherine Siena*. Translated by Algar Thorold. Rockford, IL: TAN Books and Publishers, Inc. 1974

Jean Baptiste. Chautard, O.C.S.O. *The Soul of The Apostolate*. Charlotte, NC: TAN Books. 2008

Anne Costa. *Healing Promises – The Essential Guide to the Sacred Heart*. Cincinnati, OH. Servant. 2017

Mother Louise Margaret Claret. *The Book of Infinite Love*. TAN Books and Publishers: Charlotte, NC. 2009

Father John Croiset, S.J. *Devotion to the Sacred Heart*
https://archive.org/details/devotiontosacre00croigoog

Saint Josemarie Escriva. *Christ Is Passing By.* London/New York: Scepter Publishers. 1974

Saint Josemarie Escriva. *The Way.* London/New York: Scepter Publishers. 2001

Walter Farrell, O.P., S.T.M. and Martin Healy, S.T.D. *My Way of Life.* Brooklyn, NY: Confraternity of the Precious Blood. 1952

Father Lukas Etlin, O.S.B. *The Holy Eucharist Our All.* Charlotte, NC; TAN Publishers. 1999

Saint Peter Eymard. *How to Get More Out of Holy Communion.* Manchester, NH: Sophia Institute Press. 2000

Saint Peter Eymard. *My Eucharistic Day.* Libertyville, IL. Marytown Press. 2005

Father Frederick Faber. *The Blessed Sacrament.* Charlotte, NC; TAN Books. 1978

Saint Maria Faustina. Kowalska. *The Dairy of St. Maria Faustina Kowalska: Divine Mercy in My Soul.* Stockbridge, MA: Marian Press. 2007

Father Gabriel of Saint Mary Magdalen, O.C.D. *Divine Intimacy: Meditations on the Interior Life for Every Day of the Liturgical Year.* © Monastero S. Giuseppe - Carmelitane Scalze, published by Baronius Press, www.baroniuspress.com

Ven. Louis of Granada, O.P. *Summa of a Christian Life.* Rockford, IL: TAN Books. 1979

Winfrid Herbst, S.D.S. *Eucharistic Whisperings.* Wauwatosa, WI. Society of the Divine Savior. Out of print. Available on CD. 2009

Winfrid Herbst, S.D.S. *The Way to God.* Wauwatosa, WI. Society of the Divine Savior. 1947. Out of print

Pope John XXIII (Saint). *Journal of a Soul - Autobiography of Pope John XXIII. New York, NY:* Image. 1999

Louis Kaczmarek. *Hidden Treasure.* Fort Wayne, IN: Trinity Communications. 1990

John A. Kane. *Transforming Your Life Through the Eucharist.* Manchester, NH: Sophia Institute Press. 1999

Alphonsus. Liguori. *Introduction to the Devout Life.* Rockford, IL: TAN Books and Publishers.

Alphonsus Liguori. *The Holy Eucharist.* Brooklyn, NY: Redemptorists. 1934

Alphonsus Liguori. *Visits to the Blessed Sacrament and the Blessed Virgin Mary.* Rockford, IL: TAN Books and Publishers, Inc. 2001

Lawrence G., Lovasik. SVD. *A Novena of Holy Communions.* Rockford, IL: TAN Books and Publishers, Inc. 1995

Therese Liseux. *The Autobiography of St. Therese Lisieux.* Translated by John Beevers. New York, NY: Doubleday. 1957

Martin Lucia, SS.CC. *Rosary Mediations from Mother Teresa of Calcutta - Loving Jesus with The Heart of Mary.* Plattsburgh, NY: Missionaries of the Blessed Sacrament. 1984

Stefano M Manelli. *Jesus Our Eucharistic Lord.* New Bedford, MA: Academy of the Immaculate. 2002

Blessed Columba Marmion. *Christ, The Life of the Soul.* Colorado Springs, CO: Zaccheus Press. 2005

Blessed Mary of Agreda. *The Mystical City of God* - Charlotte, NC: TAN Books. 2009

Josefa Menendez. *The Way of Divine Love.* Rockford, IL: TAN Books and Publishers, Inc. 1981

Mother Mary Loyola. *Coram Sanctissimo.* Lisle, IL: St. Augustine Academy Press. 2012

Father Anselm Moynihan. O.P. *The Presence of God.* New Hope, KY: New Hope Publications. 2012

Father Michael Muller. C.S.S.R., *The Blessed Eucharist.* Veritas Splendor Publications. 2013

Paul O'Sullivan, O.P. *All About Angels.* Charlotte, NC. TAN Books and Publishers, Inc. 1990

Anthony J. Paone. S.J. *My Daily Bread.* Brooklyn, NY: Confraternity of the Precious Blood .1954

Father Florian Racine. *Could You Not Watch with Me One Hour-How to Cultivate a Deeper Relationship with the Lord through Eucharistic Adoration.* San Francisco, CA: Ignatius Press. 2014

Rev. M. Raymond, O.C.S.O. *God, A Woman and The Way.* Milwaukee, WI: The Bruce Publishing Company. 1954

Most Reverend Athanasius Schneider. *Dominus Est – It is the Lord!* Pine Beach, NJ. Newman House Press. 2009

Federico Suarez. *The Sacrifice of the Altar.* London/New York. Scepter. Publishers. 1990

The Poor Clares of Perpetual Adoration. *Manual for Eucharistic Adoration.* Charlotte, NC; TAN Books. 2016

Jose Guadalupe Trevino. *The Holy Eucharist. Milwaukee, WI:* The Bruce Publishing Company. 1947

About the Author

Michael Seagriff practiced law for 30 years, as a general practitioner, prosecutor, criminal defense attorney and Administrative Law Judge.

His vocation as a Lay Dominican created an insatiable desire to learn, study, live and share his Faith. For more than ten years he led a Prison Ministry program and has spent more than fifteen years promoting Perpetual Eucharistic Adoration, serving as coordinator of that devotion in his former parish. He always wanted to write and share these experiences but never seemed to have the time when he was working. All that changed unexpectedly in 2009 when he retired.

Articles that he has written since retiring have been published in *Homiletic & Pastoral Review*, *The Catholic Sun*, a weekly diocesan newspaper, and on *Catholic Exchange.com* *CatholicLane.com*, *Catholic Online.com*, *Catholic Writers Guild Blog*, and *Zenit.org*.

The author acquired his healthy sense of humor and his love for the Catholic Faith from his deceased Dad and Mom and employs both frequently, sometimes to the joy and at other times to the consternation of those closest to him.

He blogs at:
http://harvestingthefruitsofcontemplation.blogspot.com/
and **http://forgottentruthsto** set faith afire.blogspot.com/
and mseagrif@wordpress.com

Other Books By Author

[The Catholic Writer's Guild awarded its Seal of Approval to *Forgotten Truths to Set Faith Afire! Words to Challenge, Inspire and Instruct* and to *I Thirst For Your Love.*]

Forgotten Truths To Set Faith Afire! Words To Challenge, Inspire and Instruct

This is a compilation of over 1200 essential but *Forgotten Truths* that opened the author's eyes, spoke to his heart and stirred his soul. The power of these words changed his life and can do the same for all read and reflect upon them.

I Thirst For Your Love

Our Lord thirsts for our love. He is waiting for us to love Him! Why have so many of us been unwilling to quench His thirst? If we really believed Jesus Christ was truly here with us, we would visit Him. Nothing would prevent us from doing so. We would not permit anyone or anything to take precedence over Him. But we do not come as we ought because not enough of us believe He is here!

It is the author's hope that after reading *I Thirst For Your Love,* you will quench His thirst, and Love! Reverence! and Visit Him!

Fleeting Glimpses of The Silly, Sentimental and Sublime

This book is a mini-memoir containing 20 of the author's personal memories and reflections that he hopes will bring you laughter at a time you feel forlorn, comfort when you are overburdened with the challenges of daily living, tears of joy when certain words you read or images they generate resurrect thoughts of those you loved and lost, greater appreciation for the gift of life, zeal for the salvation of your soul, and an increased desire to give to God and those He created what He and they deserve.

Pondering Tidbits of Truth (Volume 1) (Volume 2) (Volume 3) and (Volume 4)

These books recognize two realities of contemporary life: we are all busy people and many of us have convinced ourselves that we simply do not have the time to read, ponder and reflect on the wealth of spiritual wisdom our Catholic Church has accumulated over the centuries. Yet, we owe God and ourselves this reflective time.

There are 1440 minutes in each day. Give God just five of them.

Use one of these books every day and slowly read and chew on just one of the 100 quotations, truths and challenges it contains. Ask God to let you know how He wants you to respond to what you are reading. Then do as He tells you!

38895339R00106

Made in the USA
Middletown, DE
17 March 2019